MW00484459

# Perfect
# Love

## Lucia Hur

I am dedicating this book to the two men who have changed my destiny and shaped me into who I am today. My lifetime partner, husband, and love of my life, John, and our son Bobby.

# www.mascotbooks.com

*Perfect Love*

©2019 Lucia Hur. All Rights Reserved. No part of this publication may be reproduced, stored in a retrieval system or transmitted in any form by any means electronic, mechanical, or photocopying, recording or otherwise without the permission of the author.

This book is not intended as a substitute for the medical advice of physicians. The author and publisher do not assume and hereby disclaim any liability to any party for any loss, damage, or disruption caused by errors or omissions, whether such errors or omissions result from negligence, accident, or any other cause. The author has re-created events in this story from memory, and may have changed some identifying characteristics and details such as physical properties, occupations, and places of residence.

**For more information, please contact:**
Mascot Books
620 Herndon Parkway, Suite 320
Herndon, VA 20170
info@mascotbooks.com

Library of Congress Control Number: 2019900883

CPSIA Code: PRFRE0519A
ISBN-13: 978-1-64307-409-2

Printed in Canada

# Perfect Love

Lucia Hur

# FOREWORD

Traumatic brain injury (also known as TBI) is the leading cause of morbidity and mortality among young people in developed countries. This silent epidemic is increasing; the World Health Organization predicts that TBI and motor vehicle collisions will be the third-highest cause of disease and injury worldwide by 2020.

Traumatic brain injury affects both the individual and his or her immediate family and friends. The severity of the brain injury, the age of the individual, and the care he or she receives acutely and during the rehab phase of recovery will determine the individual's eventual outcome and prognosis. Numerous studies have shown that strong family support is one of the key factors in optimizing one's rehab potential. This was proven to be true for the Hur family.

At the present time, there is no proven treatment for TBI. Certainly, various protocols have been established, in both the acute hospital setting and the rehabilitation phase, which looks to improve outcomes; however, no single treatment has been deemed to be superior over others.

Evidence-based medicine indicates that admission to a trauma center that is well versed in the acute care of brain-injured individuals will have a positive influence on outcome and prognosis. Much has been learned recently about the acute care of the brain-injured. Previously, high-dose steroids were used to reduce elevated intracranial pressure. We now know that steroids have been associated with increased mortality rates in TBI and therefore are contraindicated in the acute care setting. Mannitol (osmotic diuretic) and hypertonic saline are the recommended interventions used to lower increased intracranial pressure. Other treatment options such as progesterone, hypothermia (cooling the body down for several days), and various antioxidants have not been shown to be effective in altering outcomes.

During the rehabilitation phase of recovery, numerous pharmacologic agents have been shown to provide some benefit. Amantadine, a dopamine agonist frequently used to treat Parkinson's disease, has been shown to improve the rate of functional recovery in individuals who are minimally responsive or in a vegetative state. Numerous stimulants such as modafinil, dextroamphetamine, and methylphenidate have shown some benefit in enhancing attention in individuals with TBI, but no positive benefit was found in regard to memory or processing speed. All of these are recent findings in neuroscience research.

The central nervous system has the ability to compensate and adapt to injury, thanks to the phenomenon of neuroplasticity. Neuroplasticity is defined as the ability for neuronal circuits to make adaptive changes, both on a structural and functional level, in response to environmental, behavioral, and neural changes. In other words, the brain can rewire itself to compensate for injury and disease. We used to think of neuroplasticity only when talking about the "young brain"; however, we now know that neuronal plasticity takes place throughout life. This is knowledge that was unavailable to the Hurs after Bobby's accident; information on TBI was in its infancy in the early 1990s.

Following an injury, neuronal plasticity occurs in three stages: 1) acutely, neuronal cell death takes place, which in turn decreases cortical inhibitory pathways and allows new, secondary pathways to develop; 2) the cortical pathways then become excitatory, which promotes new cell proliferation and revascularization; and 3) weeks after injury, axonal sprouting begins, which allows for remodeling of the damaged circuits, and the beginning of recovery. Bobby went through these three stages during his recovery.

The approach to rehabilitation of the brain-injured individual involves repetition, repetition, and more repetition. Consistent daily therapies, provided by a multidisciplinary team in a rehab setting, take advantage of the phenomenon of neuroplasticity, thus maximizing the individual's chance of meaningful neurological recovery. The brain injury rehab team, composed of the physical therapist, occupational therapist, speech therapist, neuropsychologist, social worker, physician, case manager, dietician, and, of course, family members, plays a vital role in the recovery process. Bobby had access to such a team at his rehab center.

The road to recovery following a significant brain injury is not always a smooth one. Setbacks are expected, especially when the individual has other comorbidities to deal with such as tracheostomies, feeding tubes, recurrent bladder infections, and pressure sores.

Once discharged from the rehabilitation facility, the individual will either go home or be sent to a residential brain injury facility or skilled nursing facility, depending on the individual's level of functioning. When discharged home, the family assumes a key role in the care of the individual. They discover fairly quickly that the "new normal" is both rewarding and challenging, as the individual will continue to improve long after his or her brain injury. Although textbooks assert that recovery usually maxes out from twelve to eighteen months post injury, I have seen individuals continue to make gains as far out as ten years post injury. But at the time of Bobby's injury, twelve to eighteen months was the accepted standard.

My passion and calling to care for the brain-injured individual started back in the early 1990s, the "pre-internet" days. As rehab specialists dealing with TBI, we treated individuals with various "coma cocktails" and other therapies, based on anecdotal evidence and networking among physicians. Over time, protocols were established and newer treatments emerged such as botulinum toxin injections, serial casting, baclofen pump implantation for spasticity, and constraint therapy for severe hemineglect.

It was in the early 1990s that I first met Bobby Hur and his family. Bobby had suffered a severe traumatic brain injury, which left him comatose for approximately three months. He was transferred from the acute care hospital in Lubbock, Texas to a local rehabilitation hospital in Austin. Initially, Bobby was minimally responsive and, while he remained in a comatose state, was totally dependent on others for all activities of daily living. Over the next several months, Bobby started to "emerge" and become aware of his surroundings. Aggressive therapy was provided by a dedicated multidisciplinary team that worked relentlessly to maximize his recovery. Milestones were achieved as Bobby started talking, moving his paralyzed side, and, eventually, walking.

He improved to the point that he attended and graduated from college. At the time, I didn't know of any other survivor of a severe TBI who had done so. He is now living independently, and I continue to follow him on an outpatient basis. I look forward to his visits and enjoy catching up with him.

After almost thirty years of practicing medicine and caring for the brain-injured individual, I have come to the following conclusions:

Never say never. Oftentimes, during the acute phase of injury in those individuals with severe TBI, the medical staff will encourage withdrawing care and halting further aggressive therapy. The young TBI individual deserves a chance at rehabilitation. Obviously, each case is different, and second opinions are recommended when the family is asked to withdraw care. The Hur family sought me out for such a second opinion.

The family plays a vital role in the recovery process. Bobby's parents and family members played a significant role in his rehab and ultimate recovery. They offered encouragement, participated in hands-on therapy, and were eager to learn whatever it took to help their loved one. They became an integral part of the medical team.

Do your homework before going to a rehab facility or entering a post-acute brain injury program, the way the Hurs did by visiting with me and touring our facility. Not all programs offer quality care or provide cutting-edge technology to maximize the individual's recovery. I recommend visiting the facility unannounced for a tour. This way, you see the true picture of the staff and how they deal with the individual's concerns.

Individual and family education is crucial in understanding the process of brain injury rehabilitation. It is the responsibility of the physician and therapists to share their knowledge with the family and the individual when dealing with TBI, and to encourage the family to seek answers, as the Hurs did.

A spiritual foundation based on faith and hope can make this burdensome journey less painful when the recovery process becomes overwhelming.

Never have I seen so much faith and hope come from one family as I did with the Hurs during Bobby's injury and recovery. I truly feel blessed to have been Bobby Hur's physician over the last twenty years. Hopefully, this book will offer some guidance and encouragement to those who have been affected by TBI.

David Morledge, M.D.
Austin Neurological Clinic
Director, Brain Injury Program at Texas Neuro Rehab

# AUTHOR'S NOTE

The story you are about to read is true. I should know. I am not only the author, but I am also the mother who has had to endure what no parent should ever have to endure: the report of your child being involved in a horrific car accident, which resulted in a traumatic brain injury. It transformed Bobby Hur from a young man of vitality and health into an unconscious shadow of his former self whom some medical professionals dismissed as a hopeless case. Such was the unofficial prognosis of my son, a young man of physical prowess and intellectual promise. Bobby was literally on his way from high school to college when his world—and mine—forever turned upside down.

My original intent in writing this book—which is based on a log I started to keep soon after that dreadful accident more than two decades ago—was to make it a first-person narrative, told from my own perspective. After all, since the day of the accident, I have been Bobby's primary caregiver. The problem was that putting the story in the first person shifted the book's primary focus, making it more about me than about Bobby and his heroic struggle to regain his rightful place in society. The first-person format also served to diminish the key role my husband, John, played in all of this. He may not have been on the front lines to the extent that I was, but the comfort and support and wise counsel he provided me daily was critical. Our ongoing love story is another essential element of this book.

To make this book less of a memoir and more of a narrative, I switched the voice to the third person. Some names of people and places have either been changed or omitted to protect the innocent, as well as the guilty. In the same vein, the dialogue presented here may not have been the actual dialogue spoken in a particular moment since it is difficult to recall, verbatim, conversations that took place so many years ago. Nonetheless, the spirit of those conversations has never been compromised.

This book is not meant to serve as a definitive guide on how to nurse someone back from the depths of disease and despair. Every case is different and everyone reacts to a given situation, no matter how soul-shattering it may be, in his or her own way. The chapters that follow portray how I was able to accomplish that task back then and continue to do so in the present.

This is my story. Yours may be quite different. But however different it may be, I urge you to follow this one piece of Churchillian advice: never give up. Never, ever give up. While that adage may seem self-evident and even trite, I guarantee that it lies at the heart of every successful recovery.

I have learned a number of lessons as a result of what happened on that fateful day, two of which are worth sharing here. The first is that what's important—what truly matters in this life—has little to do with the destination and almost everything to do with the journey. For example, it doesn't really matter where you end up in your career, be it high or low on the corporate ladder. Rather, what matters is the love and loyalty you express on your way. Second, the age-old adage "Nothing good ever comes easy" is true. Certainly, for me, the steps on this journey have not been easy ones. As a consequence, I have grown as a human and spiritual being. I believe the same thing can be said for my husband and for our two sons.

I hope you enjoy reading this book. More to the point, I hope you find it meaningful and inspirational. May it bring even a slight ray of hope and light to where there is now only darkness.

Lucia Hur
Austin, Texas, January 2018

# PREFACE: JUNE 4, 1994

Bobby Hur never knew what hit him. Or, rather, what he hit.

Seven hours earlier, at the start of another hot and sunny day in Central Texas, Bobby had loaded his belongings and his pet dog into his Jeep Cherokee and set off from his home in Austin. He was bound first to Lubbock, where he planned to visit his older brother, Peter, a student at Texas Tech University, then to Colorado Springs, a picturesque city nestled within the eastern edges of the foothills of the Southern Rocky Mountains.

Bobby loved Colorado Springs. He knew it well, and was eager to get to know it even better. He had spent several summers there as a volunteer counselor at the summer Christian camp, and he planned to do so again this summer. The difference was that this time, after his work at the camp was completed, he would not return to Texas. He would instead join the freshman class at the Colorado Springs campus of the University of Colorado. A new chapter of his life was about to unfold, and Bobby couldn't wait for it to begin.

Like most incoming freshmen, Bobby was both nervous and excited about beginning this new chapter. He had performed well academically at his Austin high school, and at 6-foot-1 and 200 pounds, he had excelled under those fierce Friday-night lights of Texas high school football. As a young man of Korean-American descent, he proved to his classmates that he wasn't much different from them. He was popular among both his male and female peers. Since many things came easily to him, he had every reason to believe that college would be a natural and thrilling extension of high school. It would provide him with what he would need—

academically, emotionally, and socially—to excel in all his pursuits, including whatever he chose as a career.

At the moment, though, he wasn't thinking about a career or what would happen four years later. Bobby's thoughts were full of hope and promise as he cruised northwest from Austin along Highway 84/Slaton through the vast flatlands of north-central Texas. Instead of switching on the car's air conditioning, he drove with the windows open. The hot, dry air was soothing on his skin and helped keep him awake. He had gotten precious little sleep the past few nights. After all, he was leaving behind family, friends, and colleagues he would not see again until Christmas, and he had much to say to them—and they to him. Beer and conversation had flowed easily, and Bobby had felt a rush of affection and nostalgia as he said goodbye to everyone and everything he held dear.

Once he got on the road, however, his thoughts turned to the excitement of the present and the promise of the future. Halfway into the drive to Lubbock, Bobby began feeling the first wisps of drowsiness. Although he fought them off, his mind kept nagging at him to stop and rest, and perhaps even spend the night at a motel. But his heart told him to do otherwise. He wanted to see Peter. He wanted his two days in Lubbock with his brother, and then he wanted to get on to Colorado Springs and start this new phase of his life.

"What do you think, Belle?" he asked his pet dog, a mixed Labrador. "Stop for the night? Or continue on?"

Belle was sitting up in the passenger's seat, looking around. At the sound of Bobby's voice, she turned to face him and smiled broadly. Or so it seemed to Bobby.

"Right, then," Bobby said, returning the smile. "We continue on. Give it three more hours. We should be there well before supper."

What happened seven miles south of Lubbock remains unclear. Likely, the waves of fatigue Bobby had been fighting off for the past several hours finally engulfed him. He dozed off in the hot Texas sun, and his Jeep careened down a steeply inclined road onto a grassy shoulder, bouncing along at high speed until it slammed into a roadside electrical pole with such impact that the horrifying sound could be heard in distant homes.

When rescuers arrived at the scene a few minutes later, they found a vehicle so crushed and disfigured it was barely identifiable as a Jeep. Far worse, the driver was so torn and covered in blood, the body was hardly recognizable as a human being. The electric pole had somehow ripped through metal into the middle of what was left of the car, and had trapped Bobby's leg, which was grotesquely contorted beside a mass of red pulp that vaguely resembled the body of a dog. Although the "Jaws of Life" ultimately were able to free him, when Bobby was finally placed in an ambulance and rushed to University Medical Center (UMC), no one at the scene gave him much chance.

"Poor bastard," one paramedic was heard to say. "No one can survive a crash like that. No one."

A second paramedic nodded. "If he does survive," he said, "God help him. He'll wish to hell he hadn't."

Off to the side, at the edge of the highway by a pickup truck, an elderly couple looked on silently. The man had his arm around the woman's shoulders while she wept quietly into a handkerchief.

# CHAPTER 1

Lucia Hur was getting ready for the night on the town that she had been looking forward to for a long while. Yet something was wrong. Something kept niggling at her. And it would not leave her be.

She paused to think about what it might be. Her youngest son had left early that morning, and by now should be in Lubbock with Peter. She loved the thought of her two sons being together, reminiscing about old times one moment, dreaming about the future the next. Perhaps that was what was bothering her, she thought. With both boys gone off to college, she and her husband, John, were about to experience the so-called empty nest syndrome. Many of their friends had already arrived at this milestone, and for the most part they'd had good things to say about it. Of course, you will miss your children and of course the house will seem empty for a while, they told her, but think of the freedom you'll have, the opportunities to do what parental responsibilities have prevented you from doing for so long. Besides, these friends went on to say, your children will be home for holidays. And you can always visit them at college. So, as our children would say, "It's all good."

Comforted by such thoughts, Lucia continued getting ready for the evening, a night organized by their friends Mike and Dee: a celebratory dinner, Mike had called it, at a new restaurant in town, followed by a movie. Three more sets of friends and married couples, Ed and Julie, Bob and Shirley, and Todd and Patti, would join them.

Mike and Dee were happy empty nesters. Their son Neil was a friend of Peter's. They had attended the same high school together, and now Neil and Peter were students at Texas Tech and worked part-time as paramedics at UMC in Lubbock. The thought of Peter and Bobby meeting up with Neil tomorrow comforted Lucia as she dressed for the evening. She smiled. Life was good. Everything was falling into place, as it should.

She found the perfect pair of shoes to go with her dress, and was putting them on when she heard the shrill ring of the front doorbell.

"Could you get that, honey?" John called out to her from across the room. "I'm just out of the shower."

Lucia wondered who would come calling at such an inconvenient hour. She and John were accustomed to entertaining people at odd times of day, but usually such visitors were friends or acquaintances of their sons. And this evening their sons weren't here.

When Lucia opened the door, she was surprised to see Mike and Dee.

"What are you doing here?" Lucia exclaimed. "It's only five o'clock. I thought we were supposed to pick you up in an hour."

"You were," Mike said quietly. "Plans have changed."

"How so?"

Dee drew a breath. "There's been an accident."

"An accident? Where?"

"In Lubbock."

"Neil?" This was Lucia's immediate concern. "Is Neil all right?"

Dee shook her head slowly. "It's not Neil, Lucia. It's Bobby."

"Bobby?" Lucia heard herself ask. She felt a wave of nausea. "Bobby?"

"I'm afraid so," Mike said. "We don't know all the details. But we'll fill you in on what we do know on the way to the airport. We've booked a flight to Lubbock for the four of us. We need to leave right away. Okay?"

"Okay."

"I'll help you pack," Dee said.

In a haze, Lucia followed Dee to the bedroom. A woman of action and resolve, Lucia set to work organizing for the unplanned trip. As she did so, her hands shook and her mind struggled to make sense of it all as it whirled with questions: What had happened? Where did it happen? When and how did it happen? Who identified Bobby?

"Neil confirmed it," Mike said shortly afterwards in the car. He was driving and Dee was sitting beside him. Lucia and John were in the back seat. "He was volunteering in the ER when Bobby was brought in on a gurney. Bobby was so covered in blood, at first Neil didn't recognize him."

"So how did he know it was Bobby?" John asked. He had been quieter than usual since Lucia and Dee had broken the news to him.

"Bobby was wearing his friendship ring," Mike replied, referring to the ring Bobby wore as a token of friendship with his best friend, Charles Kean. "Neil knows that ring. The whole school knows that ring and what it signifies. Bobby's initials are engraved on it. When Neil saw it, he wiped the blood off Bobby's face. That's when Neil knew it was Bobby for sure, and that's when he called us."

"I see," John said softly.

Mike's cell phone rang. "Hi, Neil," he said. "Mom and I are in the car with Bobby's parents. We're on our way to the airport." He listened. "Yes, of course you can speak to her."

Mike handed the phone to Lucia.

"Hello, Neil?" Lucia said. "How is Bobby?" She listened while Neil spoke quickly. "Oh, I see. Yes, of course you have our permission. Please do it. We'll be there as soon as we can."

"What did he say?" John asked as Lucia handed the phone back to Mike.

"Our permission," Lucia said simply. She looked out the car window at nothing.

"Permission for what?"

"For Bobby to receive immediate surgery. Neil is signing on our behalf. He is trying to get ahold of Peter."

"I see," John said.

They passed the one-hour flight in silence. At the airport in Lubbock, Neil and Peter picked them up in two cars, and then they all sped off to the hospital.

It was nine o'clock in the evening, Day One.

"How bad is it?" Lucia asked Neil in the waiting area. John had gone off with Peter to check on Bobby's condition. When Neil was slow to respond, Lucia said, "Can you at least tell me what time the surgery began?"

"They had already begun preparations by the time I called you," Neil said. "The surgery began soon after that."

Lucia had enough medical knowledge to realize that an ongoing surgical procedure in the emergency room that had already lasted four hours indicated something very dire, even life-threatening. Again, Lucia felt nausea rising; her limbs began to tremble.

She sat down and buried her face in her hands. Neil, Mike, and Dee sat in silence.

When John and Peter rejoined them in the waiting room, their faces were devoid of expression. They both went out of the way to avoid eye contact with Lucia.

"How is he, for God's sake?" Lucia demanded. "He's going to be all right, isn't he?"

John Hur is not a man who tells lies, not even white lies to make his wife feel better. He believes that truth is always best, no matter how painful. And John, who knows his wife, realizes that while she can be short-tempered and impatient, she is calm but determined in a crisis.

"It's bad, Lucia," he said. "Worse than we imagined. One doctor said it's a miracle that Bobby is still alive."

"*What?* Oh my God, John!" Lucia wailed. "How can this be? How badly is he hurt? Where does he hurt?"

"Just about everywhere. His legs are in rough shape, but their major concern is damage to his brain. It's dangerous to operate when the brain is damaged. So, we have to prepare ourselves for the worst. In fact, the doctors are saying that the surgery might not do much good."

Lucia got up and buried her head against her husband's shoulder. She felt as though she might faint, and, for once, took little comfort in John's firm embrace.

"What are we going to do, John?" she said. "What are we going to do?"

"Pray," John said.

As the minutes stretched into hours without any definitive word from the hospital's medical staff, Lucia reached deep inside to draw upon a strength she had often relied upon to see her through difficult times. That strength was now being tested.

Although not Bobby's biological mother, she had been a mother to him in every other sense of the word since he was a preschooler. She loved him dearly.

And Lucia loved John, a man who had suffered far too much already. He had already been through this horror once with his first wife, Susan, Peter and Bobby's biological mother. Now he had to, once again, accept the unacceptable, and Lucia knew better than anyone the toll all this would take on him.

She had to be strong—for Bobby, for John, for Peter. Lucia had always been the strong one. John was the stable one. They had often told one another that they made an unbeatable team. As Lucia kept vigil that night in the silence of the waiting area, she wondered if that strength could continue to hold the family together, if it could even, perhaps, save Bobby's life.

Finally, at one forty in the morning, Neil told them that the surgery was over. It had lasted nine hours. "Bobby will be transferred to the intensive care unit soon," he said.

"When can we see him?" John asked.

"That's up to the doctor," Neil said. "He'll be out soon. He's a good man and an excellent surgeon. I can vouch for him."

"You already have, Neil," Lucia said. "And I know his reputation."

Twenty minutes later the neurosurgeon walked into the waiting room.

"The surgery went well," he said. "But there are complications."

"Will Bobby wake up soon?" John asked.

The surgeon shook his head slowly.

"It's hard to tell anything at this point," he said. "There's been considerable damage to the brain."

Lucia's resolve to remain calm began to slip. She stepped close to the doctor and asked, in a voice that was both accusatory and pleading, "Surely you have seen many cases like this in your practice. So, can't you at least give us some idea of where we are here? Do you not understand our despair in knowing nothing?"

"I do understand, Mrs. Hur," he said in a thoroughly professional tone. "It's just too soon to know anything definitive. We have to give it a few days." With that, he turned and headed for the door.

"When can I see Bobby?" Lucia called after him.

"Soon. I'll let you know," the doctor said.

"Why wouldn't he give me a direct answer?" Lucia muttered in frustration. "And what did he mean by giving it a few days? I wasn't asking for anything definitive. I was just asking for his thoughts, that's all."

Dee put her arm around Lucia's shoulder.

"It's going to be all right," she said. "It's going to be all right, you'll see. Just give it a little time."

But for Lucia and John, time was a commodity in short supply.

A few minutes later Neil announced he had to return to work in the emergency room. He handed the keys to his apartment to his father, saying that Bobby's parents could stay there as long as necessary. He knew Peter had a roommate, leaving him not enough space to host his parents.

"Thank you, Neil," John said earnestly. "We appreciate your kindness very much."

Neil nodded and left.

"You go check into a hotel and get some sleep now," Lucia said to Mike and Dee. Fatigue was written across their faces. "I'm afraid I must insist on that. You've done everything you could possibly have done, and now you need some rest. John and I will call you if need be."

Reluctantly, Mike and Dee complied. When they were gone, Lucia turned to her elder son.

"Tell me who discovered the accident."

Peter massaged his eyes and forehead.

"An elderly couple, local farmers, driving behind Bobby saw the accident and called 911," he said. "It happened only seven miles from Lubbock, so the paramedics got there in a few minutes. The couple followed the ambulance to the hospital. They left only when they were sure that Bobby was inside and in good hands."

"Did you get their name and address? I would like to personally thank them."

"Sorry, Mom. I didn't," he said. "Mom?"

"What is it, Peter?"

"I feel terrible that this happened. I feel partly to blame for it. He was coming to see me, right?"

Lucia took her son's hand and squeezed it. She looked deep into his teary eyes.

"You are not responsible, Peter," she said quietly. "Not at all. Sometimes things happen that are out of our control. This is one of them."

She was about to say more when the door to the waiting room opened and a man walked in. It was Bobby's surgeon.

"Mr. and Mrs. Hur," he said, "Bobby is being transferred to the intensive care unit. You can see him soon. It will take some time to get him settled, so may I suggest you get a couple of hours sleep. The sun will be up soon enough."

John glanced up from where he was sitting.

"Thank you, Doctor," he said, and then stared back down at the floor.

There was no point in glancing in his wife's direction. They both knew there would be no sleep for either of them tonight.

# CHAPTER 2

For the next several hours, Lucia prayed. Raised in the Catholic faith, she prayed to the God of her upbringing and to everything holy in the universe.

"You brought my son into this world for a purpose," she prayed to the Almighty, "but he has not yet fulfilled that purpose. Please give him another chance, I beseech you. Do not take him like this. He still has much to do."

"Amen," John said from the couch beside her.

John had his eyes closed, and Lucia understood why. In times of great stress and challenge, he often closed his eyes to transport himself away from where he was and into a deep sleep to escape such a nightmare, if only for a few minutes. Lucia had often seen him do this. From the time she had first met him, soon after the untimely death of his first wife, Susan, John had often lapsed into periods of despair and silence. As a youth, John had come to the United States to get a college education. Having little money and no credit or professional references, he had to scramble to support himself and fight his way through college. After graduation, he went through several positions in small companies until he finally landed a dream job as an engineer for IBM. He had left that job not long before Bobby's accident and taken a full-time position as a real estate developer and investor, something in which he had only dabbled previously.

Lucia had already witnessed the ups and downs of the entrepreneurial lifestyle. Before moving to Austin in 1985, John, who was a private investor at the time, had made several trips there to explore real estate investments. At the time, the real estate market was better in Texas than just about anywhere else in the States. The Hurs made a huge investment, which was a great success—at least at first. It was during John's second attempt as a full-time entrepreneur that the market crashed, and everything came tumbling down. As cruel fate had it, this was also the year of Bobby's car accident.

"It will be all right, honey," she would say to her husband at such times. "It will be all right." How she wished that someone would say those comforting words to her at this moment and with confidence.

Between prayers for Bobby that night, Lucia prayed for John. She knew well what effects the injuries to his son were having on him. She also prayed to God to give her strength. She, too, had her demons to pacify.

A young girl of vision and promise, she had left Korea at the age of seven and gone to Malaysia, where her father had been invited to work as a surgeon and help train other doctors, as well as open medical labs. In Malaysia she attended an international convent school. Her innate love for learning coupled with her perfectionist father who made his children memorize one-hundred English words a day helped Lucia to learn the language quickly. Initially, she thought to follow in her father's and brother's footsteps and pursue a medical career, but she had to abandon that idea when she discovered she couldn't stomach the sight of blood.

That night, in the waiting room, Lucia clasped her hands together and prayed that God would look over her and keep her alive to be there for her husband and sons.

Eventually she drifted off into a restless sleep.

A while later, Peter gently shook her awake.

"Mom," he said. "We can see Bobby in a few minutes."

Lucia opened her eyes to see Peter and Neil standing there beside Mike and Dee. Judging from their bloodshot eyes, no one had gotten much sleep. Through the window, the first rays of morning sun filtered into the room.

Mike handed Lucia and John Styrofoam cups of coffee and breakfast sandwiches. John accepted both and started eating, but Lucia took only the coffee.

"Try to eat something, Lucia," Dee urged. "You need to keep up your strength. We're all relying on your strength."

"There'll be plenty of time for that later," Lucia said. She couldn't eat anything. Her stomach was twisting more than ever. "Let's go."

"Mrs. Hur," Neil said as they made their way toward the ICU, "be aware that Bobby is all bandaged up as a result of the surgery. And he's in a coma."

"I know the drill," she said.

"I know you do," Neil said. "I'm just trying to minimize the shock."

But nothing could have prepared Lucia and John for the sight that confronted them. Due to the risk of germs and contamination, they were not allowed entry to the intensive care unit. Instead they had to observe their son through a window, and what they saw looked to them like a gruesome cross between an ancient Egyptian mummy and a robot. Bobby's entire body—if indeed that was Bobby—was covered in white gauze, with openings only for his eyes, mouth, and nose. From head to toe a myriad of tubes and wires, going in and coming out of him, monitored vital statistics via a host of machines surrounding his bed. Only the figure's height and bulk suggested that the being within those tightly bound bandages might indeed be their son, Bobby Hur; a living being with a living heart.

"Oh, dear God," Lucia said softly. When she felt her husband wrap his arm around her waist, she leaned into him. "Oh, dear God."

"It's all right," John whispered to her. "It's going to be all right."

Lucia looked over at him. His lips were tight, his eyes were watery, and his skin bore the pale gray of deep despair. At that moment she felt a surge of love and resolve wash through her.

"Yes," she vowed. "Yes, it will."


The initial diagnosis by Bobby's surgeon seemed to believe that burst of confidence and optimism. The accident, he told Lucia and John the next day, had damaged the front part of Bobby's brain. The extent of the damage could not be determined at this point, he said. To discover the extent, they would need to conduct a series of tests in the days to follow. But of this they were sure: Bobby's cognitive powers and memory had been severely compromised.

"How soon will we know something definitive?" Lucia asked.

"As I indicated," the surgeon said, "I can't answer that question at the moment. We'll just have to wait and see."

How long will he be in a coma?" John asked.

"Could be days, or it could be weeks or even months," the surgeon replied. "We'll have to wait and see."

With precious little to do, Lucia and John had no choice but to wait and see.

On the second day after the surgery their friends Bob and Shirley came from Austin to visit at the hospital. In an act of unselfish love, they had driven seven straight hours in the Hur family Suburban because they thought Lucia and John would appreciate having their own car in Lubbock.

Bob and Shirley insisted on staying for a few days but Lucia politely said no; they had done enough, more than could possibly be expected even from best friends. Her rational side kicking in, Lucia knew that the presence of friends and family, however well-intentioned they might be, could at times be more of a hindrance than a help. With that in mind, she urged them to return home with Mike and Dee.

Lucia had a lot of work ahead of her. John would help, of course, but the burden would fall on her. Coming from an academically oriented family, she would conduct all the research necessary to learn everything she could about brain trauma and healing.

There was a second great challenge, beyond helping to restore her son to life: Lucia had an industrial chemical manufacturing company to run. While that business had great future potential, it needed a lot of hands-on work and management to generate income, as limited as it was. Regardless, hospital bills were already mounting. Lucia had to keep the cash flowing  since the company's income had become the major source of the Hurs' household expenses. John was struggling to get his real estate empire back on its feet, but that was going to take a while.

With a strong background in sciences and a master's degree from University College London, Lucia was able to apply her skills to formulate and produce products with the help of John, who also held a postgraduate degree. The problem was that she had no formal training in sales or marketing strategies, or, for that matter, any other business discipline, including finance and accounting.

The concept of "effective promotion" to increase sales was, at first, a mystery to her. Since her business was small and she couldn't delegate PR responsibilities to other workers, she did everything. When she and John attended conventions, Lucia became a one-person show. Taking charge of the company booth, she began at six in the morning most days and continued well into the night talking to potential customers, handing out free samples, giving product demos, and delivering educational seminars.

There was no one Lucia could hand work off to; hers was a one-man show, as evidenced by a telephone conversation several months back with a disgruntled customer. When she was unable to solve the issue to the customer's satisfaction, he demanded to speak to the sales manager.

"I am the sales manager," Lucia said.

A pause. "Then I would like to speak with the R&D manager," he said.

"I am the R&D manager," Lucia said.

Another pause. "Put me through to the CEO," he demanded.

"I am the CEO," Lucia said.

Another pause, more pronounced this time.

"But you're a female," he blurted out.

"You're right, I am."

"But companies like yours do not have female executive officers," he said with exasperation.

"This one does," Lucia said with finality.

What the customer did not know was that Lucia was petrified whenever the phone rang, and was often relieved to the point of tears when a call ended. She was, at first, that unsure of her own abilities; talking was not her forte.

Finally, after many years of hard work, Lucia succeeded in turning the company around. Cash flow improved to where she could afford to hire a production assistant and bring payables in line.

But she had not yet reached that point during Bobby's initial comatose months. Although they could now see a hopeful light at the end of the tunnel, the light was but a prick and remained far away. Their financial position was tenuous, their future unclear.

First things first, however. Priority number one was Bobby and his pathway back to full health and recovery.

That was assuming such a pathway existed.

# CHAPTER 3

The hours grew into days and the days went beyond a week. Bobby's condition remained unchanged. He lay still on his back in a deep sleep, his heavily bandaged chest rising and falling almost imperceptibly. Every few hours John entered his room in the ICU to shift Bobby's position enough to avoid bedsores and to increase his circulation by rubbing and massaging his limbs. John and Lucia were by his side almost constantly, talking to him, holding his bandaged hands, trying desperately to offer healing and comfort in any way they could.

These questions became Lucia's new mantra when their son's primary doctors could not provide satisfactory answers.

"Doctor, is there really nothing you can do?" Lucia asked for maybe the thousandth time. "Do you have any idea how difficult this all is for my family?"

"I do understand," the doctor replied in a tone that was both professional and sympathetic. "I'm sorry, but we are doing all we can do."

"And what is that?"

"Keeping him comfortable and hydrated and his vital signs closely monitored."

Lucia already knew the answer to her next question but asked it anyway.

"Have you noticed any changes in his vital signs? Any indication that he may soon be coming out of the coma?"

"None as of yet."

Lucia slowly shook her head. "How long are you prepared to wait and do nothing?"

"As long as necessary. Bobby is in a very serious coma. To try to force anything at this stage could bring serious consequences."

Lucia again shook her head but said nothing further.

By now Lucia had installed a fax machine and a telephone in Bobby's room, in order to run her business from the hospital. The business—life itself, essentially—had to go on; she and John would soon be awash in unpayable medical bills and other expenses. But it was almost impossible to focus on running a business. When her portable cell phone rang, she would have to leave Bobby and take the call-in a nearby room. If it was a customer complaining about a product or haggling over a price, she had to swallow her pride and anger, and negotiate as though that customer was her only concern in the world. It was a bitter pill to swallow. She felt guilty for taking those calls, but there was no way around it. Talking casually to customers as if nothing out of the ordinary had happened to her and her family was among the most difficult thing she ever had to do.

Bobby, meanwhile, slept peacefully, as though he would never wake up. When not attending to business matters, Lucia was either at his side or learning everything she could on inducing someone out of a coma and coma stimulation.

At night Lucia continued to pray to God, although her words were at times mixed with confusion and even resentment. She simply could not understand how God could allow such a horrible thing to happen to such a wonderful young man.

She also prayed to Susan, Bobby's biological mother. A devoted nurse and mother, Susan was struck down in the prime of her life by the cruelest of fates: a police cruiser, for unknown reasons, ran into her car as she was getting off work after the graveyard shift. A quadriplegic from then on, Susan lived for another three years. Bobby was only three years old at the time of Susan's accident. In a real sense he never knew his biological mother. Nevertheless, Lucia knew that Susan cared deeply about her sons and John. She considered Susan her sister-in-spirit and asked for her love and guidance.

During the first week, Bobby appeared to be in a peaceful rest, as if merely meditating. But as more time passed, he began to slump and appear heavier, as if slipping into an ever deeper and more consuming sleep.

Lucia's anger intensified. Once again, she expressed her frustration to one of Bobby's doctors.

"Why is it that Bobby is going into a deeper and deeper sleep?" she pressed. *"Why?"*

When the doctor offered what was by now his stock response— "We'll just have to wait and see"—Lucia resolved to become more proactive in her son's recovery. Lucia knew that the patient's family had a right to access records, charts, and other documents, especially when the patient was under twenty-one years old. Doctors were rarely enthusiastic about releasing such documentation, but they had no legal right to withhold it.

So, Lucia insisted on seeing her son's medical records and charts to draw her own conclusions. Gathering this information was no easy task since Bobby had one team of doctors taking care of him during the day, another team at night, and several interns and residents throughout the day. To complicate matters, the information was difficult to interpret without the aid of medical expertise.

For example, different doctors gave Bobby different doses of anti-seizure medications, and nothing in the medical records indicated how these decisions were being made. What was worse, none of the procedures and outcomes were discussed with Lucia or John. No one is closer to a young patient than his or her parents. To keep the parents out of the loop and in a fog when their child's life is on the line seemed beyond explanation. At times, Lucia had to alert a doctor or nurse to the proper dose—oversights that would have never come to light had she not been so diligent 24/7.

Furthermore, Bobby's doctors did not seem interested in conferring with each other. They came into his room—usually individually—to scan the data and make whatever changes they deemed appropriate. And then they left John and Lucia sitting there, wondering.

One day, while doing her own scanning of the charts, Lucia found that Bobby was being given one bolus (a large dose delivered in a short period of time to reach a therapeutic level quickly) of an anti-seizure medication called Dilantin (phenytoin)—the first line of defense in an ICU to maintain a patient's vital signs and stability. Lucia discovered that this medication, as a side effect, makes the patient drowsy and sleepy. Some are more susceptible than others. So as more doses were given, Bobby drifted into a deeper and deeper sleep. This made no sense to Lucia. She believed that Bobby needed to be stimulated, not induced into *a deeper* sleep. And anyway, how does a doctor determine the proper dose when he or she cannot measure the drug's effectiveness because the patient is sleeping constantly? Lucia expressed her concerns about this medication to his doctor.

"Why would you not change the current anti-seizure medication to something that does not put Bobby into a deeper sleep?" she wanted to know.

The expression on the doctor's face indicated his displeasure with the question.

"As I believe I have told you before, Mrs. Hur," he said, "your son has suffered a serious shock to the brain. Any seizure he might have at this point could be very dangerous. I am treating him with this medication because I believe it is the most effective medication in preventing any such seizure."

"I'm sorry, Doctor, but I don't agree with you," she said. "I understand that Dilantin (phenytoin) can be effective initially, but I believe the time has come to try something different. Switch to another anti-seizure medication. I believe we should get Bobby out of the coma as soon as possible. Since we cannot do anything until he wakes up, waking him up should be our top priority."

The doctor decided not to argue further. It was a typical response. None of Bobby's doctors seemed to know what to do about Bobby's condition. Keeping him alive and comfortable was the extent of what they seemed willing and able to do. John and Lucia felt helpless, since all they could do was massage their son's arms and legs, which was not enough to wake him. How long would this go on?

Lucia resolved to do more research to find out all she could about traumatic brain injuries and how best to treat them. This was no easy task, considering that the World Wide Web was still in its infancy and precious little information was known about TBI.

# CHAPTER 4

Lucia mulled over her research, weighing how what she learned connected with Bobby's situation. For instance, the human brain, which weighs from three to four pounds and consists of extremely delicate tissue floating in a ball of fluid, is not only protected by the skull, but also three layers of membranes. According to one source she found, traumatic injury occurs when an exterior physical force impacts the brain and causes the patient's life to change dramatically and, in most cases, devastatingly. Although in-depth analyses had not been conducted at the time of Bobby's injury, it was widely believed by medical professionals that the most common cause of TBI was a car crash (an example of a closed-head injury), followed by a gunshot wound to the head (an example of an open-head injury). It cannot be caused by anything internal such as a tumor, stroke, or a prolonged lack of oxygen to the brain. In Bobby's case, he was diagnosed with a closed-head injury, and more specifically a diffuse axonal injury (DAI) which affected the six broad areas of functioning.

TBI can be mild to severe depending on such factors as:
Duration of unconsciousness

Force of impact to the brain and skull

Location of impact on the brain

Duration of time the brain is without oxygen flow

How quickly the patient receives hospital care

Duration of sleep/coma

Lucia focused her research strictly on the most severe causes and effects of a closed-head injury.

In a closed-head injury such as Bobby's, the head comes to a full and sudden stop after moving at a high rate of speed. Such an impact causes the brain to move forward and back—and/or from side to side—causing the brain to collide with the bony skull surrounding it. This violent jarring bruises the delicate brain tissue, thereby stretching and tearing axons and neurons, and tearing blood vessels. Damage to axons is of particular concern, for they are the parts of a neuron (or nerve cell) along which impulses from one cell body are conducted to other cells. Axons are thus used by the brain for communication purposes; they are what make us all "tick." Everything our brain does for us depends on the proper communication between axons and neurons.

After a closed-head injury, damage to the brain can be confined to a specific area (localized injury) or throughout the brain (diffuse axonal injury or DAI). Initially, Bobby's doctors believed that the damage to his brain was not a DAI. DAI is a brain injury in which damage in the form of extensive lesions in white matter tracts occurs in a widespread area. DAI is one of the most common types of severe traumatic brain injury. Since Bobby was in a persistent vegetative state of unconsciousness for months, his doctors should have assumed that DAI had occurred.

Lucia's research also revealed that while the primary injuries in, for example, a car crash can be quickly diagnosed, a number of secondary injuries can occur after the onset of TBI, and it is the prevention of these secondary injuries that a hospital medical team works to prevent when the patient is first brought to the emergency room. These injuries may be caused by oxygen not reaching the brain, either because of low blood pressure or by brain tissue swelling. If any of these secondary injuries occur, the delicate chemistry of neurotransmitters can be further compromised, leading to further complications as time passes.

As Lucia and John would soon discover for themselves, the long-term effects of TBI can be both challenging and devastating, especially as these effects alter and distort one's fundamental character.

For the moment, however, they refused to dwell on the future. Instead, they clung to a ray of hope provided by a phenomenon known as the plasticity of the brain, or neuroplasticity.

The brain is a dynamic organ that has an inherent ability to adapt and heal itself. Even after catastrophic damage, it can readapt by establishing new connections and means of communication between neurons that carry messages within the brain. In fact, the brain can create new neurons within certain parts of the brain. Furthermore, plasticity of the brain is more likely to occur when the brain is active rather than dormant. Readaptation rarely occurs without some sort of exposure that prompts the brain to get to work. Changes do not happen quickly, however, which is why rehabilitation can take months or even years before significant improvements are realized.

Gradual rewiring, readaptation, and self-healing could occur within Bobby's brain, given proper external stimulation. This knowledge gave Lucia and John immense hope. While holding on to this hope, one question still remained: how do we get him out of his coma?

During Bobby's vegetative state at UMC, he had measured at under a three on the Glasgow Coma Scale, a fifteen-point scale based on motor, verbal, and eye-movement responses of comatose patients. A score of three indicates an ominous status: severe disability.

"Why don't you start a coma stimulation therapy?" Lucia asked one of Bobby's primary doctors. Urgency accompanied her question once she thoroughly researched the topic. She was not trying to be confrontational, however. Despite their mounting frustration over their son's treatment—or lack thereof—Lucia and John continued to hold the medical profession in high regard. It was, after all, Lucia's own heritage. But sitting back and being content to "wait and see" had become unacceptable to them both.

"That kind of treatment cannot be given to a patient while he's in the ICU," the doctor said. "He must first be transferred to another unit."

"Then why don't we do that?" Lucia said with as much composure as she could manage. "Transfer him to another unit."

The doctor frowned.

"Your son is in a coma." His voice edged on exasperation. "A very serious coma, as you know well. To move him from ICU now could be dangerous."

"I understand that, Doctor," Lucia said. "But my husband and I have done our research, and we believe that something needs to be done other than hoping and eternal waiting. Bobby needs to wake up. Only then does he have a chance to come out of the coma and fight. The time has come to start coma stimulation!"

"We'll just have to wait and see, Mrs. Hur," the doctor said again, forcing Lucia to use whatever powers she had to keep herself calm.

"I am very disappointed with modern medicine," she confided to her husband that evening. "We seem to know so little about how to get someone out of a coma." For one of the first times in her life she regretted her decision not to pursue a medical career like her father and brother who became doctors.

Each morning Lucia woke up hoping against hope that this would be the day Bobby would open his eyes, smile up at her from his bed, and say those two sweet words: "Hi, Mom." But each day she was disappointed to the point of tears. One morning, three weeks after the surgery, Lucia and John were summoned into the office of the neurologist who was in charge of Bobby's care post-surgery.

The doctor politely bid them good morning, then motioned to them to sit on the sofa facing her desk. After she sat down, she clasped her hands before her as if in prayer. When she spoke, her voice was as solemn as her expression.

"Mr. and Mrs. Hur," she said, "I asked to see you this morning because I believe it's time, we face certain realities, however difficult these realities may be. To state it bluntly, my colleagues and I have concluded that it is now highly unlikely that Bobby will regain consciousness. We all regret this, but we all concur. Yes, it's true that there are cases of patients who suddenly come out of a coma after one or even two months. But this is not the norm. It is, in fact, very rare. And even when it does happen, the patient normally suffers severe memory loss along with a number of other defects. More than likely, he or she will end up living in a vegetative state. We believe that this, unfortunately, is the most likely scenario for Bobby, assuming he is able to come out of his coma eventually."

The neurosurgeon sat back and gazed intently at Lucia and John. Her eyes were not unsympathetic. Perhaps, Lucia thought, she truly did feel sorry for all that had happened. But in those same eyes was a steely resolve to end the matter. It was as though she had grown bored with this case and was keen to move on to a different patient and a different set of parents.

Lucia went cold. She felt the familiar, sickly twist in her stomach. She opened her mouth to speak but could not.

John spoke for her.

"Are you giving up just like that," he asked, "without really trying?"

"It's not a question of giving up, Mr. Hur," the doctor responded. "As I said, it's a question of accepting realities. As long as your son is in our care, we will never give up trying to help him. But I must repeat the obvious. It will take a miracle for your son to recover, and it's time to prepare yourselves to face some cruel realities."

"I happen to believe in miracles," Lucia said. "Do you?"

Before the doctor could respond, Lucia rose to her feet. To her mind, this conversation was over. The doctor's words had not deterred her. In fact, she was now more determined than ever to see Bobby recover and lead a normal life; she would do whatever it took, even if that meant moving heaven and earth to get the job done.

"John," Lucia said after they returned to the privacy of Bobby's room. "We can't rely on those doctors for Bobby's life. They've already given up on him. We need to do this in our own way. We need to do whatever it takes to get him out of here. We need to find a new hospital for him."

Lucia sat down. The fire had gone out of her temporarily. She gazed upon her son lying on the bed, a young man of nineteen years, so full of fortitude, intelligence, and promise. He was a star football player of such prowess and willpower. No challenge seemed to daunt him. His peers looked to him to lead the way. People of all ages liked and admired him. How could such a strong and competent young man not awaken from a coma and rejoin the living?

"We must not give up on him, John," she said softly. "That must never, never happen."

She was not certain why she felt the need to say that. Perhaps she was concerned that John may have accepted what the doctor had told them a few minutes earlier. This she was sure of: John loved his son and worried endlessly about him. But he also loved his wife and worried about her. What John said next seemed to confirm her doubts.

"I want you to think long and hard about this," he said to her. "I will go along with whatever you decide. But what you're proposing won't be easy for any of us. It could be particularly hard on you."

Lucia bit her lower lip.

"I realize that, John. But don't worry about me. I can take it. Besides, what's the alternative? Giving in to the doctors here and giving up on Bobby? We can't do that, ever. Bobby is a tough kid. He can take this, and so can you and I. We have to rely on ourselves until we can find a new hospital for him."

John nodded slowly while looking deep into Lucia's eyes. They were brimming with tears, as were his. He held her hands but said nothing. He didn't have to. How he felt about Lucia, how he felt about Bobby, how sorry he was for the financial difficulties forced upon them by the real estate market crash, Lucia still carrying the burden of having to operate a chemical manufacturing company to support the family, what they now had to go through together to save their son—all of that and so much more was written in bold script in the lines upon his face.

"We'll make it," Lucia said as she squeezed his hands. "We'll survive all this, the four of us: you, me, Bobby, and Peter. We'll all be a regular family once again. Trust me."

"I do trust you, Lucia," John said. "And I thank God for you."

# CHAPTER 5

The search for a new hospital began the next day. What Lucia and John wanted was a hospital near their home in Austin. Such a location would reduce travel time and logistical challenges, which in turn would give them more time with Bobby and also time for both of them to do their work. Cash flow remained a critical issue, and they had no safety net. Generating income would be the only way to pay the mounting medical bills and other expenses.

The paramount issue, however, was finding the right doctor for Bobby. That meant finding a doctor who was ready, willing, and able to think outside the box. What they did not want was a doctor steeped in traditional medicine who would not use innovative thinking or treatment methodologies—the sort of doctor who went by the book. They had experienced that sort of doctor here in Lubbock, and while they continued to believe that its medical staff was competent, this wasn't the right hospital for Bobby. They needed a doctor who understood how they felt and who would be open to working closely with them toward Bobby's recovery.

Lucia set about making a list of doctors based in the Austin area, taking careful note of their education, experience, patient reviews, and other qualifications, and started calling them one at a time. She told each of them what had happened to her son, and what she and her husband expected from a doctor. Their sole request was that the doctor would include Lucia and John in the process of treating Bobby. They did not want to be mere observers of what Bobby was experiencing; they wanted instead to play a proactive role in his treatment and recovery. They wanted to be a part of the medical team.

Several well-known doctors in Austin made it very clear very quickly that they would not allow Lucia and John to participate. According to these doctors, Lucia and John should leave everything to the professionals—the one thing Lucia would not tolerate anymore.

"Why is this, John?" she lamented one evening. "Why won't they let us be on the team? We have so much to contribute."

"Perhaps," John said, "it's a matter of liability mixed with professional pride. They can't bring themselves to accept that a lay person can contribute much."

"I am hardly a lay person when it comes to medicine," Lucia said.

"I know that," John said. "But they don't know it. Not yet. They'll learn."

After a number of days and dozens of telephone calls, the Hurs got the break they were looking for. HealthSouth Rehabilitation Hospital of Austin met most of their criteria, including the most important one: Dr. David Morledge, a young neurologist who was not only passionate about his profession and innovative on how best to practice it, but also expressed keen interest in Bobby's case.

He did throw out the caveat that before he would accept Lucia's conditions, he would need to consult with his team and receive permission from the hospital administration to have her and John admitted as part of the medical team.

The depths of the gratitude John and Lucia immediately felt for Dr. Morledge was impossible to articulate. They might have believed it had they been told he was an angel sent from heaven.

Lucia did not hear anything from the doctor for a week; she and John were on pins and needles. She knew in her heart that this hospital and this doctor were right for her son. Would the powers-that-be put yet another roadblock in their path? She prayed hard every day. On the seventh day her prayers were answered when she received a telephone call from the hospital.

"They said yes, John," she said softly as she put down her phone. "They said they want to talk to us."

No promises were made. No plan was set in stone. But at least now they had hope.

Lucia put her face in her hands and wept.


Despite the good news, there remained the issue of having their son moved from a hospital in Lubbock to one in Austin. It's not as if they could just buy him a seat on a plane.

First Lucia and John had to fly home to Austin, leaving Bobby in Lubbock for several days. They wanted to check out Health-South Rehab, and meet the medical staff to discuss Bobby's case before he was transferred. A month had passed since they had flown to Lubbock with Mike and Dee, although it seemed like many lifetimes. So much had transpired since that fateful day that even the familiar landscape of their hometown seemed foreign to them. They both felt as though they had been through a time warp.

The HealthSouth medical team asked Lucia for a detailed description of Bobby's accident, his current condition, and as much information about his treatment to date as she was able to offer. After a long meeting during which few stones were left unturned, Lucia and John were invited to step outside while the medical team and hospital administration conferred among themselves. Again, Lucia felt a nauseating flutter of dread in her stomach.

At length, the medical team and Dr. Morledge emerged to say that they had agreed unanimously to admit Bobby. Lucia thanked them profusely, unable to conceal her immense relief and overwhelming sense of excitement.

"Lucia, honey, listen to me," John cautioned once they were alone. Worried about what he believed was over-exuberance, he put his arm around her shoulders and looked into her tear-filled eyes. "You mustn't get overwrought," he said. "This is only the beginning. We have a long, long road ahead of us. We need to be prepared for that."

"You're right, John," she said, wiping her eyes. "Of course, you're right. But what we have now is hope. *Real* hope. And I'm hanging on to it for dear life."

That afternoon, Lucia and John flew back to Lubbock and went straight to the hospital. After looking in on Bobby, they informed hospital administrators that they would be moving Bobby to Austin. They already knew that a seven-hour car ride and traveling via a commercial airline were out of the question. Because medical personnel had to accompany Bobby every step of the way, the only option was an air ambulance. All that stood in the way was Bobby's doctor, who had to sign off on the transfer.

The doctor did not seem the least bit surprised by what Lucia had proposed, which led Lucia to believe that somehow the hospital had gotten wind of her intentions.

"I'm sorry, Mrs. Hur," the doctor said. "I cannot do that. Not at this time."

"Why on earth not?" Lucia demanded. "You said yourself that there was no hope for Bobby in this hospital. All we're doing is moving him to another hospital that holds out hope for him. Why would you not sign off on that?"

The doctor folded her arms.

"The patient is not stable at the moment and is therefore at risk," she said. "If anything were to happen to him during the transfer, the hospital would be responsible and therefore liable. I simply cannot and will not accept that responsibility."

Further arguing with the doctor and hospital administration proved fruitless. The next day, after consulting with a lawyer, Lucia and John returned with a different proposition.

"What if my husband and I, as Bobby's parents, assume full responsibility for the transfer? We will sign the necessary papers stating that under no circumstances will we hold the hospital accountable for anything that may happen. Will that appease you?"

The hospital administrators reluctantly agreed because they had no choice, but they stressed again how risky and dangerous the transfer could be to Bobby, and they urged Lucia and John to reconsider their decision. Although they listened respectfully, they remained as adamant as ever to get their son moved to a new location. Besides, Lucia was too excited, too full of joy and hope, to remain angry for long.

In the midst of Lucia's excitement another problem arose: the expense of an air ambulance, especially when the doctor does not recommend that the patient be transported. Since Lucia and John's insurance carrier would not cover the cost toward this crippling expense, the bill wore their pockets even thinner.

They had no choice—it was do or die. And there was no time to waste on useless squabbling.

The air ambulance was already landing on the roof of the hospital when Bobby's parents completed the necessary paperwork. But just then, Bobby's temperature spiked. The hospital insisted they wait until his temperature came down. They claimed it was too dangerous to transfer him in his present condition. With no time to think it over, Lucia had to make what was perhaps the most difficult decision of her life. They could not wait forever. Nor was there any guarantee that Bobby's temperature would be stabilized any time soon.

Lucia looked at John.

"We're going," she said, and John nodded.

The staff at the hospital, however, refused to budge. Time was rapidly ticking away. Since arguing with them—or begging—seemed to be fruitless, Lucia asked Peter to ask a different doctor, an acquaintance of Peter's, to intervene on their behalf. This doctor, the same one who had performed the initial surgery, reviewed Bobby's charts, asked the Hurs to sign an additional form accepting all responsibility for Bobby's welfare post-release, and then let them go.

Lucia and John had finally overcome a major obstacle keeping them from what they believed was the best possible treatment for their son. But, as John had predicted, other obstacles were on the horizon.

# CHAPTER 6

John and Lucia were not allowed to accompany their son in the air ambulance; only the patient and one medical staff member were permitted on board. John and Lucia had to drive to Austin. As soon as possible, they loaded their six weeks' worth of belongings and acquisitions—including boxes of medical textbooks, journals, and magazines on TBI—into their vehicle and headed for home. It was the beginning of the new leg of their journey.

While John drove, Lucia sat in the passenger seat and stared out the window at the passing scenery. It was not the farmhouses, small towns, or herds of longhorn cattle grazing in the pastures and fields that captured her attention during the seven-hour drive. It was her memories of Bobby as a child; as a bashful preschooler who had blossomed into a popular and boisterous young man who loved to write and draw; as a stalwart member of his varsity high school team on those Friday nights; and as a son who made his parents proud. Yet, here he was, being transferred from one hospital to another, his life hanging in the balance. He deserved none of this. His father deserved none of this. Neither did his brother, Peter.

Lucia felt utterly overwhelmed by it all: her son involved in a near-fatal car crash, followed by a nine-hour surgery and a deep coma. It frustrated her to no end that in spite of her immense research on TBI, the medical staff had essentially given up on him. What a turn of events when Lucia found a new hospital and a new treatment methodology. While this was a breath of fresh air for the first time in weeks, the truth of the matter was that the hard work was about to begin—the new treatment followed by who knew how many months or even years of rehabilitation.

On the flip side, Lucia's chemical business had to go on. She had to remain in daily contact with her customers, vendors, freight companies, and her staff—those responsible for getting the products out while she felt utterly gutted by the tragedy that had befallen her son and her family. The hardest part of her daily routine was to put on a brave face. There could be no flaws, no screwups, no dissatisfied customers. Cash flow had to continue, because until John was able to restore his real estate business, the responsibility for the family's financial survival lay squarely on Lucia's shoulders.

While it all seemed to be too much to handle, there was one thing she learned from this experience: when life is this nightmarish, this despairing, this soul-destroying, even crying becomes difficult. With that, Lucia would not allow herself to wallow in sorrow or self-pity. She knew she had to remain calm, strong, and resolved.

"Is everything okay, honey?" John asked at one point during the drive.

Lucia shrugged.

"I was just thinking about Bobby," she confessed. "I'm worried about his temperature. Maybe the doctors back there were right."

"Stop worrying about that," John said. "Bobby is fine. He's with a medical staff member who is watching over him constantly. We made the right decision. Now try to get some rest."

But rest for Lucia was out the question. Insomnia had long been an issue in her life, and it had only gotten worse in recent months. Now she found it difficult to get to sleep without her prescription sleeping pills. She knew these pills could be addictive, but she also knew that a serious and sustained lack of sleep was a bigger issue.

Just as Lucia had shut her eyes to try to get some rest, Mike called the car phone from the hospital in Austin.

"The air ambulance is here," he said. "Bobby is being admitted as we speak. Dee and I are standing by."

"How is he?" John asked.

"Seems to be fine. No worries for the moment. We'll see you here when you get in."

The look John and Lucia exchanged after the call said it all. Mike was not only Bobby's godfather, he was like a brother to John, just as Dee was like a sister to Lucia. They were blessed beyond words to have such loyal and devoted friends.

Halfway through the trip they stopped for gas and to switch drivers. John was asleep the moment they pulled out of the gas station. Lucia envied her husband's ability to sleep no matter the situation. It was a man's way of escaping the misery of despair, she thought, just as tears are often a woman's response. Once again, she felt a wave of admiration for her husband. He was such a strong, reliable, and dependable man, one who kept his emotions close to his heart. Above all, he had integrity. When the real estate crash hit Texas and devastated the value of John's properties, he could have saved many of them by declaring bankruptcy. But that would have meant stiffing the bankers who had worked closely with him over many years, and this was something John refused to do. Instead he swallowed huge losses and debts.

Lucia loved John for doing what she thought was the right and honorable thing, and for so many other reasons as well. She knew he loved his son. But she also knew that he loved her too, and deeply. If push came to shove and they had to make a life-or-death choice for Bobby, Lucia was positive John would make the right decision.

*But it must never come to that,* she resolved as they drove toward Austin. Now that Bobby was where he should be, with proactive doctors, Lucia was determined to focus all of her efforts on bringing Bobby out of his coma. Once that happened, the healing could begin.

Several hours later they drove into Austin. It was good for them both to be back in familiar territory, among people they knew and places they had been before. They were home.

"I suggest we go to the house first," John said from the passenger seat. "We can unload our stuff, take a shower and change, and then go to the hospital."

"Good idea, honey, but no," Lucia replied. "We're going straight to the hospital. Mike and Dee are waiting for us. Not to mention Bobby."

Mike and Dee were indeed waiting for them in the waiting room when John and Lucia arrived at the hospital. Dee jumped up and raced over to give Lucia a hug.

"You look wonderful," she said. "A little skinnier than before, but wonderful." Her eyes brimmed with tears, as did Lucia's, although she tried to blink them away.

"You'll have to wait until tomorrow to speak with the doctors," Mike said. "I've taken the liberty of booking a meeting with them for ten in the morning. But for tonight, they've gone home, which is what I suggest you two do. You both look done in."

"Can we see Bobby first?" Lucia said.

"You can. I've already made arrangements with the head nurse."

Lucia squeezed his arm. "You're a gem, Mike. Thank you."

Bobby had been placed in a nicely appointed, rather spacious private room on an upper floor of the hospital. He lay on his back, gently sleeping. He was hooked up to all the tubes and wires and computers he had been back in Lubbock. In fact, it all seemed somewhat surreal to Lucia. From the room in Lubbock to this one in Austin, nothing had changed but the décor. Secretly, she had hoped that the transfer from one hospital to another might somehow have jolted Bobby out of his coma. That hope, she realized now, had been nothing more than wishful thinking. Nothing really had changed, at least not yet.

As they all left together, Dee said, "You'll need to arrange for a caretaker, won't you?"

"No," Lucia said. "No caretaker."

"But you and John both have to work," Dee insisted. "How can you work and take care of Bobby?"

"We'll manage," Lucia said. "We're the ones responsible for Bobby's recovery. No one else, including the doctors. We will assume full responsibility."

Dee let the conversation end. She knew Lucia well enough not to try to change her mind once she had made a decision.

John and Lucia arrived at the hospital thirty minutes before their scheduled meeting the next morning. Feeling both excited and afraid, Lucia wanted to be there early so she might have some quiet time to think and meditate first, which helped her to calm her heart and steel her mind. She knew from experience that there were many dispassionate and irresponsible doctors out there. But she also knew there were doctors like her father—those who truly cared about their patients and did their best to do everything they could for them. She prayed that the doctors who would be caring for her son were cut from the latter cloth.

Despite their thirty minutes of serenity, both John and Lucia walked into the meeting room with some trepidation. There to greet them were eight members of a medical team, headed by the young neurologist Dr. Morledge and rounded out by another doctor, two shift nurses, and various therapists specializing in specific areas of traumatic brain injuries.

After a round of introductions and pleasantries, the Hurs were invited to recap the series of events since the car crash. John stood up, and in that quiet and unassuming yet comprehensive way of his, he recounted the facts as he and Lucia understood them. He stressed what had happened at the hospital in Lubbock and why he and his wife felt compelled to find a new hospital staff and a new method of treatment for their son, both of which he most earnestly prayed they had found in this room.

When John sat down, Lucia rose to her feet. She looked directly at the young neurologist.

"I want to add to what my husband just told you," she said. "It's imperative for you to understand why we complained to the doctors at Lubbock about giving Bobby the anti-seizure medications, Dilantin (phenytoin) and Phenobarb (phenobarbital). We understand the need for the anti-seizure medication in times of trauma, and its importance in the ICU. However, in Lubbock they administered it continuously, without any meaningful result except plunging Bobby into a deeper sleep. They were giving Bobby one bolus dose after another without checking his tolerance levels or his level of sleep. His Glasgow scale number dipped to three."

She looked at John for a quick boost of strength and continued.

"We were convinced that these medications were only causing Bobby to sleep more heavily," she said, "and, thus, slip into a deeper coma. This made no sense to us."

She then rehashed some of the conversations with the Lubbock doctors.

"I had the distinct impression," she said, "more from what they *didn't* tell us that they didn't know what else to do, except to keep to their default procedures. Furthermore, since the role of intensive care is only to pursue stability, it was never their goal to initiate coma stimulation."

Lucia slowly looked around the table, making sure she made eye contact with each person.

"John and I believe that Bobby needs coma stimulation therapy. Immediately," she affirmed. "I want his doctors to understand how we feel and do the best they can to help Bobby regain consciousness. We encourage you to be innovative and experimental. I seriously doubt Bobby's condition can get much worse, so why not try something different, something creative, something that, God willing, is more effective? We won't blame the hospital if a new treatment doesn't work. We will take full responsibility. But please," she said. "I beg you, try something. And please, let us be a part of the decision-making process. We have much to contribute beyond the love that any parent has for his or her child. We can help. We *want* to help. Please give us this opportunity to help save our son. For starters, there is another anti-seizure medication named Tegretol that we could try."

As Lucia finished and sat down, a stunned silence took over the room. Too much on edge to glance up at those gathered around her, she stared down at the table, even though she felt their eyes studying her.

At length, Dr. Morledge cleared his throat.

"Thank you, Mr. and Mrs. Hur," he said. "We very much appreciate everything you have told us here today. You spoke with reason and you spoke with emotion. Although we already knew much of what you said from the forms you previously filled out, hearing it from you has been most helpful.

"As I believe I have already told you, my colleagues and I believe that parents make the best doctors for their children. No doctor or nurse can know a child or attend to his needs more than a parent. That has always been the philosophy at this hospital."

Lucia glanced up. "Thank you, Doctor. May my husband and I assume that we can attend your weekly meetings and actively participate in Bobby's treatment?"

When the doctor glanced around the room with questioning eyes, he received brief nods in reply from his peers.

"Yes," he replied, "you may assume that. And we are happy to have you on board. Together we will do whatever we can to get Bobby back on his feet, so to speak."

He smiled at the Hurs.

Returning their smile, John and Lucia knew right then and there that the right decisions had been made. The bond was sealed.

# CHAPTER 7

That very day, Dr. Morledge and his medical team implemented a customized treatment plan for Bobby. First in order was to gradually shift his medication to Tegretol (carbamazepine). Lucia and John were more than pleased. They took that decision as a sign of hope and change.

Next, came coma stimulation therapy, which would provide multiple sensory stimulation to Bobby in his vegetative state. Lucia had done enough research to know that this type of therapy includes a program of intense and repetitive stimulation that has the potential of awakening comatose patients and returning them to a reasonable level of functionality. It works by activating the reticular system, a set of interconnected nuclei located throughout the brainstem and responsible for maintaining consciousness.

John and Lucia were also pleased that Dr. Morledge included massage treatment therapy in the plan. This form of therapy, which involves deep massage to the legs and arms and other parts of the body to stimulate blood circulation and to relax the muscles, is exactly what John had been doing for Bobby in Lubbock.

Lucia was encouraged to try some homeopathic treatments recommended to her by friends, family, and associates. The only stipulation was that she inform the doctors every time she administered such a treatment. Lucia readily agreed.

Lastly, Dr. Morledge would make sure that Bobby received therapeutic doses of "brain cocktail food," a mixture of different vitamins and minerals. to aid with coma stimulation.

To Lucia, Dr. Morledge's medical plan for Bobby made complete sense. Just thinking about how the medical staff in Lubbock would frown on such treatments made Lucia upset over the time wasted on passive conventional treatments. As a result, she blamed herself; she believed she should have known better.

In this way, a customized treatment plan was created for Bobby.

Despite the progress—or more accurately because of it—Lucia frequently found herself getting upset over the time wasted in Lubbock on passive conventional treatments. She blamed herself. She believed she should have known better.

"Honey," John would say at such times, "stop doing this to yourself. It just makes you upset and doesn't do any good. Stop torturing yourself over something that's already said and done."

Lucia knew that her husband was right. It rarely serves to dwell on the past. The future is important, but it's the present that truly matters. Still, although she accepted these truths, she couldn't help herself. "I am only human," she would often reply to John's entreaties, and they would leave it at that.

John gave his son a full body massage each day. Lucia tried, but weighing a mere one hundred pounds, she found it nearly impossible to lift Bobby's leg, let alone turn him. The fact that Bobby was unconscious added to the challenge. Although Bobby had lost weight during the weeks he was in a coma, he remained a strapping young man.

Even for John the full body massage was a challenge. The process demanded two to three hours, and John would need to rest for a few minutes every half hour or so. By the time the process was finished, he was often soaked in sweat and needed a short nap on the couch to recharge his batteries.

By necessity, the daily attention John and Lucia committed to their son had to accommodate their work obligations. They each had an office in the one building in Austin they still owned after they had sold off the rest of John's commercial properties. Yet they rarely ran into each other during the day. Up every morning at the crack of dawn, John would drive the forty-five minutes to the hospital to be in Bobby's room by seven thirty. At the same time, Lucia would drive the fifty-five minutes to her office to attend to the many demands of her nascent chemical business. At three thirty each afternoon, Lucia would relieve John, who would then either go home to work and prepare dinner or go to his office to work a few hours before the day was done. Each worried about the other working too hard, but both were meeting their goals and making progress. Although their cash flow burden began to ease, there was no time to enjoy the conveniences and other fruits of labor enjoyed by so many of their peers and friends.

One afternoon several weeks into this new regimen, Lucia took a close look at Bobby after John had left for work. To her eyes, Bobby looked different. He didn't look as pale as he had in previous days. The skin on his face had a healthier glow to it. And he did not appear as though he were in a deep sleep. Rather, he appeared as though he were simply taking a soothing nap.

During her study of medical journals since the accident, Lucia had concluded that just because the brain is asleep does not mean the body's senses are asleep as well. This meant that Bobby's *other* senses were functional, and that gave Lucia an idea.

She took out a bottle of perfume from her purse, opened it, and held it close to Bobby's nose. She watched his face closely. No response. But this experiment gave her another idea. The aroma of perfume sold over the counter, she thought, was not strong enough to stimulate a young man's senses—so she would concoct her own potion. She would make a super concentrate out of her industrial perfume by baking it under a Texas sun and letting the liquid evaporate, thus creating a more powerful and effective scent. *That should stimulate his olfactory senses,* she thought. She would also wrap ice in a thin cloth and apply it directly to the skin on Bobby's face. Just like a fetus in a womb reacting to a perceived threat—a natural defense mechanism widely observed throughout the animal kingdom—Bobby's body would, or at least could, react to an unexpected stab of cold.

A memory sparked yet another idea, as Lucia recalled Bobby's summers working as a volunteer counselor at the Christian camp in Colorado. He loved that job. He loved being with the kids and sharing the wonders of the Rocky Mountains with them, especially the forests rich with the heady scent of pine trees. The bark of those pine trees, Lucia speculated, would serve two critical purposes: it would stimulate both Bobby's sense of smell and his memory of happy times. He had repeatedly told Lucia how much he loved the aroma of outdoor living and, of course, the scent of the pine trees.

Immediately, she was on the phone with the camp administrator in Colorado Springs. The staff remembered Bobby well and had heard what had happened to him. Eager to lend a hand, they sent Lucia bushel baskets stuffed with pine bark and pine needles. "To one of our best and most popular counselors we've ever had," read a note attached to one of the bundles. It was signed by the camp's director.

Shortly thereafter, Lucia started a daily routine when she arrived in Bobby's room at three thirty each afternoon. Sometimes John would stay and watch. At other times doctors or nurses would stand by. The routine was simple. Lucia would try to stimulate Bobby's senses while talking quietly to him.

"Bobby," she would say, "please come back to us. We are all here waiting for you. You once told me you loved me. Please come back and show me how much you love me. That is your mother's only wish. Please come back and make it come true."

Or she would say, holding the pine bark close to his nose, "Do you remember this smell, Bobby? It's from your camp in Colorado. You love Colorado and you loved that camp. You always told me about the smell of the trees there. Here is that heavenly smell, Bobby. Breathe it in. Enjoy it. Remember those good times. Come back. Come back to us."

Each afternoon and evening she would speak like this to him in a soft, singsong tone, all the while gently trying to stimulate him. Although he showed no immediate response, she was convinced he could hear her, and so she continued doing it, often well into the night after the hospital went quiet.

As time passed with still no response, she was tempted to scream out, "Why don't you do something? Why don't you say something? Am I bothering you? If I am, tell me so!" Too often, talking to Bobby and walking down memory lane caused her eyes to fill with tears and rendered her momentarily speechless.

Days passed by. Weeks. Soon it was a month, and still no response.

*If the stimulation doesn't work,* Lucia thought to herself, *maybe I'll make Bobby so irritated he'll wake up and tell me to leave him alone.* If he did that, she knew she would weep with happiness. As it was, she wept with sadness. John worried endlessly about his wife, but was all too aware that any protests or urging for her to take it easy would fall on deaf ears.

Another week passed; another month. No response from Bobby. The doctors were now telling them that with each passing day their son's chances for recovery grew dimmer.

"Honey, are we doing the right thing?" John asked late one evening as they sat before a supper neither of them had any interest in consuming. "Is this really the best we can do? When and where does this all end?" He spoke so quietly, Lucia had to ask him to repeat his questions.

Lucia looked hard at her husband. What she saw in his eyes and written upon his face saddened her. He looked very tired. Done in. Burned out. He looked as though he had given up. Worse, he looked as though he thought everyone involved—especially Bobby—would be better off if Bobby had died in the accident. She understood. John was a quiet and proud man who used words sparingly. But his eyes and countenance spoke of the suffering he had experienced in his life, especially surrounding the death of his former wife, Susan. He cared deeply about his family, about his friends, about life. Of that there could be no question. But everyone, Lucia knew well, has a tipping point, and it looked today as if John had reached his. His bearing today was that of one who has been dealt a hammer blow to the heart and soul—twice.

Lucia steeled herself. She could not let on that she was feeling the same frustration, despair, and emptiness. She had to be strong. At least she had to *appear* strong, or else there was no hope. There was no safety net.

"John," she said, taking his hands into her own and feeling the roughness of his skin. "It seems God is testing us, and this is one test we must pass. We can't give up. Not now, not ever. What will happen to Bobby if we do? He's a tough kid. And we have to be tough, too. Who knows? Maybe he's fighting to come back even as we speak."

John nodded slowly. He then turned his head away to hide his tears.

"You're right," he managed to say. "Of course, you're right. It would be cruel beyond words to abandon Bobby now. But I hate to see you suffer so. I couldn't bear to see anything happen to you just because you came into my life."

Lucia squeezed his hands. "John, honey, don't say that. You are not doing terrible things to me. You have given me more love in this life than I thought I would ever find—love from you and Peter and Bobby. Please don't worry. I am fine. I can handle this. Okay?"

"Okay," John said.

When a couple faces hard times—especially as the result of an unexpected disaster—one of two things happens: either the couple starts blaming each other and wallowing in self-pity and then splits apart, or they close ranks and grow even closer. John and Lucia grew ever closer as the tides of misery ebbed and flowed. John loved Lucia for many reasons, not the least of which was her love for his two sons and her determination never to give up, a characteristic no doubt inherited from her father.

At the core of Lucia's love for John was the respect she had for a man who did not have the same advantages she had enjoyed, as the daughter of a successful cardiovascular surgeon, and had to work that much harder to accomplish his goals. John had arrived in the United States at the age of twenty-four virtually penniless, and he had studied hard and worked hard at three jobs, starting out washing dishes in a restaurant while living with his older brother, Michael, until he was able to get on his feet. Since he hadn't owned a car then, he took a bus to work, but due to the restaurant's late closing time he was forced to walk the two hours back to his brother's house in the pitch dark, often through the snow along ice-cold streets, his feet numb with the warning signs of impending frostbite.

Most nights, he would splash cold water onto his face when he got home and study English until almost dawn. What English he had learned in middle and high school in Korea was not sufficient to carry him far in America. As Michael had advised him when John first set foot on American soil, the first thing he had to do was to learn to speak and write effective English. Without those skills, he wouldn't go far. So, John practiced and practiced—practiced a language that belonged to another culture. Formal education came later, after he had mastered the language through sheer force of will.

This mind-numbing routine continued day after day, week after week, month after month, and year after year. John's goal, at first, was simply to survive without being a burden to anyone, including his brother. His goal, to be accomplished through time, a slightly improved financial standing, and marriage to a good woman, was to make something of himself while providing for a family.

To Lucia, John's brand of perseverance and grit was admirable to the extreme. She knew he would overcome every obstacle and personal affront—of which there were a number, given his ethnicity and his quiet, unassuming demeanor—even if some of those in her inner circle claimed that John was no great shakes and that Lucia could "do better."

John made her heart sing. He softened the rough edges of her character and her psyche, and he made her feel like a woman. A woman who is cherished. A woman who wants more than anything to give her man comfort and hope. No man had ever made her feel the way John made her feel. She had always believed in the superior powers of womanhood, but John was her match in every way. And her partner.

And that's what they both needed most now: a partner to deliver comfort and hope.

# CHAPTER 8

One month in Lubbock and now two months in Austin.

Three months since the accident.

The doctors in Lubbock had told John and Lucia that if a patient remains in a coma for a week, the chances of recovery are about 50 percent. If a month, the chances drop to 10 percent.

At three months, the number was 1 percent.

But Dr. Morledge did not deal in percentages. He had told the Hurs there is always hope, and he encouraged them to continue doing what they were doing.

"Because of it," Dr. Morledge stressed in one of the weekly meetings, "Bobby cannot be considered a 'normal' coma patient. He is exhibiting none of the numbness and sores that most bed-ridden patients display. And he has not lost his bodily functions. This is all good news. Well done. Keep it up!"

"Thank you, Doctor," John said quietly. During the past few weeks he and Lucia had come to know the medical team quite well, and vice versa. Their relationship was based on mutual respect and functioned like that of a close-knit family. "We all thank you, Bobby included."

The doctor eyed him intently.

"Let me be frank, Mr. Hur," he said evenly. "Most parents would have given up before now. But not you and Mrs. Hur. You two are different. My colleagues and I have rarely seen your ilk in this hospital, and we admire you more than you perhaps realize. You don't depend on what we tell you and leave it at that. You listen to us, but you do your own research and you follow your own heart. We are learning from you just as you are learning from us."

"You have my wife to thank for that," John said. "Not me."

"That's not true, John," Lucia said, "and you know it. Everything we do, we do together."

In the days to follow, John brought new spirit to his massage sessions with Bobby. It was as though the doctor's words had given him new life, and maybe new life for his son, too.

Lucia, however, found herself sinking inexorably into a dark ditch of depression despite her best efforts to remain calm and strong. The three-month "deadline" for coma patients had come and gone without any change, and the future seemed bleak. Her lifelong insomnia returned, worse than ever, and she lost weight to a degree that greatly worried John. But he said nothing. He had learned to remain silent on the issue of his wife's health.

Much like their son lying comatose on the bed, Lucia and John were existing, but by no one's standards were they living.

One evening, while Lucia was applying ice in a towel to Bobby's face, a night nurse entered the room. After giving Bobby a shot and checking on his intravenous feeding, she told Lucia how much she admired her persistence in trying to stimulate her son. Lucia smiled at her and confessed that she feared the hospital staff must think her weird, doing the same thing day after day without getting tangible results.

"You don't know that you're not getting results, Mrs. Hur," the nurse said. "There's always hope, and if anyone deserves to have hope, if anyone deserves a miracle, it's you."

After the nurse left the room, Lucia looked lovingly at her son.

"Wake up, Bobby," she said in her well-rehearsed, soothing voice. "You've been asleep for three months and it's time to wake up now. Open your eyes now, honey. Open your eyes and look at me."

Then she saw it.

Or did she?

It was like a small twitch on his right index finger, followed by the slightest jerk of his head away from the towel.

Then, in an instant, it was gone. When it did not happen again, Lucia dismissed it as an illusion, a figment of her imagination, a confirmation of the desperation she felt in the pit of her soul. And yet, the more she thought about what she *thought* she saw, the more convinced she became that she had seen it. She picked up the ice towel and rubbed it under his nose, a bit more aggressively this time.

"You don't like this cold towel, do you, Bobby?" she said. "Why don't you try turning away from it?"

Although she rubbed the towel under his nose for several moments more, there was no further response from her son. Buoyed nevertheless, she went out to the nurses' station to report what she had observed.

The nurse summoned a doctor and together they followed Lucia into Bobby's room. Lucia demonstrated what she had done with the ice towel, hoping against hope that Bobby would respond in some minute way. But he did not. He lay stock-still, breathing in regular motions. The doctor and nurse waited for a few minutes, and then took their leave.

"Get some rest, Mrs. Hur," the doctor said, suggesting that he attributed what Lucia thought she had seen to extreme fatigue. "I'll check in on Bobby in the morning."

Alone once again with her son, Lucia reviewed what had happened in her mind and began to suffer doubts that she had seen anything unusual. But she had, she convinced herself. She *had* seen something unusual.

She applied the ice towel a few more times, without incident. At length, she left the room and drove home. In her kitchen she told John what she had seen. John was not convinced.

"You think you saw what you saw only because it's what you desperately want to see," he said in his usual reasonable tone of voice. "I'm sorry, honey. I seriously doubt it was real. Let's get some sleep now. We both need it."

"I can't sleep, John. What I'm telling you actually happened. He twitched and tried to turn his head away from me. It was real, but no one believes me!"

"Okay, honey, okay," he said. "I believe you. Here, come with me."

He led her into the kitchen and seated her at the dining table. He then uncorked a bottle of pinot noir and poured out a glass.

"Drink this," he said, handing the glass to her. "It will help you sleep. I don't want to see you collapsing from fatigue."

Like the doctor at the hospital, John suspected that what his wife had witnessed was an illusion induced by a combination of exhaustion and a desperate need to believe. Lucia decided not to press the point further. She drank her wine and went to bed. But peace did not come easily for her that night. *Surely, the finger twitch had not been an illusion.*

The next day, Lucia left work earlier than usual and proceeded to the hospital. Before saying goodbye to her husband and sitting down beside Bobby, she conferred briefly with John and a nurse to ascertain if they had noticed anything unusual about Bobby. They hadn't. So far, the only stimulation that appeared to have worked at all was the cold towel method. This method she applied off and on for several hours, without any response from her son. Lucia left the hospital dejected, questioning anew what she had seen—or not seen—the previous evening.

Yet Lucia remained as determined as ever. The next afternoon she took her usual place in the chair beside Bobby's bed and applied the cold towel just below his nose.

"Bobby," she said, "it wasn't just my imagination, was it? You know it and I know it. You don't like this cold towel, do you? Show me how much you hate it!"

Bobby frowned, almost imperceptibly. Again, she applied the cold towel. Again, he frowned. Lucia immediately wept with joy.

"Oh Bobby, thank you!" she shouted. "Thank you! You *are* coming back!"

Instinctively, she gave her son a hug, and then laughed out loud when she realized what she was doing.

She summoned as many doctors and nurses as she was able and described to them what she had seen. The medical staff seemed somewhat perplexed both by the description and by the excitement in Lucia's voice. It occurred briefly to Lucia that they must either believe her or believe she had gone completely nuts. And when, at their request, she again applied the ice towel, Bobby showed no reaction.

The next afternoon, Lucia was once more applying the ice towel when a nurse came in to check on him. For a flash second,

Bobby frowned and tried to inch his face away. In the same instant, Lucia saw his right index finger twitch.

"Look!" Lucia cried. "Bobby just moved his head and a finger. Watch!"

Lucia applied the ice towel and again Bobby responded. This time, the nurse saw it. Immediately she summoned a doctor and all other members of the medical team who could be spared.

The nurse explained to them what she had seen. The doctor urged Lucia to apply the cold towel to Bobby's nose. The room went deathly quiet as everyone watched and waited. Then it happened—Bobby reacted the same way he had before, but with even greater movement.

"My God," the doctor murmured. "My God."

Then pandemonium broke out. The head nurse came over and hugged Lucia as everyone else broke into smiles, cheers, and handshakes.

"I'll call John," a nurse shouted.

A few minutes later the medical staff filed out of the room, leaving Lucia alone with her son. She gazed down lovingly at Bobby, too choked up to speak. In what seemed like mere minutes, John was there with her, taking her into his arms, holding her close. He, too, was too filled with emotion to speak.

"Well done, honey," he managed at length. "This is all because of you. No one else could have done this."

"We did it together, John," Lucia said. "With Bobby's help."

"This is only the beginning, the doctor told me."

"Yes, I know. Now we start with our real treatment. But that treatment is much more hopeful. At last we'll have Bobby back with us."

"We have a long way to go," John cautioned.

"Yes, we do," Lucia said.

John and Lucia spent the rest of that day and night with Bobby. Members of the medical team came and went, all of them offering congratulations. Lucia was elated; she brought in a celebratory cake and, thanking the entire team, stated that the true miracle was the coordinated efforts of an entire medical staff.

Underlying the good cheer, however, was always a note of caution.

"We're still in the early stages of recovery," Dr. Morledge said. "Please don't expect too much for a while. Expecting too much generally leads to disappointment.

"It's a miracle when a patient comes out of a coma after three months," he went on to explain. "But remember, at this stage we don't know how much of the brain and body will be functioning in a normal range, or what degree of recovery can be expected. These uncertainties are compounded by the fact that Bobby has suffered severe brain damage as a result of the accident. He may not have lost many of his cognitive abilities; on the other hand, a worst-case scenario is that he'll be in a prolonged vegetative state. So, as I said, please don't expect too much too soon. Doing so would only hamper our ongoing treatment."

Lucia looked at John. Her eyes said it all. She could not understand why the doctors were saying such things to her when she was so excited and hopeful. But she was soon to discover the answer. In the days to follow, a revolving door of doctors and nurses were in and out of Bobby's room. His vital signs and overall condition were studied hour after hour.

Lucia, meanwhile, tried to stimulate other parts of her son's body. She remained convinced that his senses were working fine, and felt strongly that such stimulation would continue to be beneficial. She tried applying the ice-cold towel to Bobby's feet. He did respond, but it took a while.

Every time Bobby seemed to be drifting off to sleep Lucia would say to him, "Bobby, open your eyes!" It scared her to see him drift off. She feared he would revert to his former comatose state, even though the doctors assured her that outcome was highly unlikely. Still, Lucia could not help herself. Even when Bobby was "awake," he had no focus. And he kept closing his eyelids, with his eyeballs continuing to flutter behind them.

"Bobby, can you hear me?" Lucia would say to him at such times. "Can you open your eyes? Open your eyes if you can hear me."

On one glorious occasion Bobby did more than he was asked. He opened his eyes and for the first time began looking around the room at the doctor and two nurses who were standing there watching. His gaze ultimately settled on his parents.

Lucia took his hand in hers. "Bobby, do you know who we are? Do you?" she asked. "Blink your eyes if you know who we are."

Bobby seemed to be staring through his mother. He showed no reaction whatsoever. But when the doctor and nurses left the room, leaving him alone with his parents, he blinked twice.

"Bobby responded, John," Lucia said. "He blinked his eyes."

Lucia may have suspected that Bobby was playing tricks, waiting for the medical staff to leave the room before doing what his mother had asked him to do. He always was a bit of a prankster, always out for a good laugh. But she knew better. Because of her research, she knew that with severe trauma to the brain, it could easily take five minutes for the brain to "digest" what was being requested of it and then send a signal to the body to respond.

From then on, Lucia and John measured the time it took to get reactions from Bobby. However frustrating it became for them both, John reminded his wife that at least they were getting a response.

"I love you, Bobby," Lucia would say to him during each of her afternoon sessions. "I love you so much. Thank you for coming back to us."

She already knew what her next mission would be: to get Bobby to sit up. After that, who knew? She felt invincible, as though Bobby could do whatever was asked of him. As though he were invincible. Certainly, it seemed as though the medical staff believed that since they were abuzz with the "miracle" that had occurred on the third floor.

News had spread outside the hospital as well. Bobby had always had many friends, and these friends, upon hearing the blessed reports of Bobby's apparent recovery, requested most fervently to visit their dear friend and offer what comfort and encouragement they could. Lucia and John continued to urge caution, however, as Bobby surely remained in a very confused state. We had no reason to believe he understood where he was or what had happened to him. To expect anything out of him, at least for now, would be futile. Austin was not Hollywood, where coma patients wake up and instantly recognize friends and family members. The dark knowledge festering in Lucia's mind was that many patients, whatever the length of their unconsciousness, never fully recover. Some remain in a vegetative state for the balance of their lives.

John and Lucia therefore told Bobby's friends to wait a while longer, in order to see what happened next. Having said that, Lucia and John were quick to express their profound gratitude for the care and concern these young men, many of them Bobby's former football teammates, had shown. The Hurs had known many of them for a long time. While in middle and high school, Bobby and Peter often brought home dozens of these teammates, all of whom seemed to have insatiable appetites and ate their hosts out of house and home. But neither Lucia nor John was ever overly concerned about that. Rather, they basked in the breadth and depth of the camaraderie they observed at such times, and took great satisfaction that these young people were safe and happy hanging out in their house.

There were other benefits, too. The parents of these young men loyally attended every Friday night football game, home or away. A close bond of fellowship and common interests bound the group of parents together, and during the previous three months the support and concern of such people had significantly helped Lucia and John to cope. Sending a note or leaving a message on an answering machine were small gestures that went a long way. Friends matter in life, and John and Lucia were blessed to have many of them.

But in the days to follow, a blanket of discouragement once again settled over John and Lucia. They had expected a slow but steady advancement in Bobby's condition, but instead they found themselves hitting a brick wall day after day as Bobby did not respond further. To anything. He lay there as though dead, his face devoid of any expression, the sole sign of life found in the blinks of his eyes. He could not sit up by himself, nor eat by himself. He could do virtually nothing by himself. His parents could not even talk in normal tones in his room, lest the noise stimulate him into a seizure, which was always a possibility with comatose patients.

"How can this be?" Lucia asked Dr. Morledge one day, the tone of her voice edged with extreme exasperation.

"It's what I told you earlier, Mrs. Hur," the doctor said. "It's why I cautioned you about being too optimistic too quickly. Bobby has suffered severe brain damage, and his brain has been out of commission for several months. It has likely lost a lot of functionality, and it certainly has lost a lot of memory. It is now like a piece of blank white paper. Our job now, and it will be a laborious one, is to start filling in the blanks."

Despite all she had suffered through and despite her extensive research into traumatic brain injury, what Dr. Morledge said left Lucia speechless.

# CHAPTER 9

It took a team of three—Lucia, John, and a nurse—to prop Bobby up in bed. He had no sense of balance, nor could he hold his head up. Once he was sitting up, a small fortress of pillows kept his head and body fixed in place.

Shortly thereafter a customized wheelchair was ordered for Bobby. It was designed, through a network of braces and thigh straps, to keep his head and body securely in place, just as the pillows did on his bed. It was motorized, and one could move it forward or backward by simply pressing the right button. Of course, Bobby had to know which button to press and how to press it. Teaching him these simple tasks proved to be a Herculean effort and therefore proceeded slowly. "One step at a time," John reminded his wife. *One step at a time.*

A more urgent matter was teaching Bobby to eat and drink. For more than three months he had been fed intravenously. Now it was time for him to learn how to swallow his food.

This, too, proved to be a mammoth effort. Every day a therapist tried to teach Bobby how to put a spoonful of soup in his mouth. She went through the motions for him, but when she put it in his mouth, more often than not the liquid would dribble down Bobby's chin onto a cloth napkin, with precious little of the substance going down his throat and into his stomach.

Lucia and John were stunned by how difficult it was to teach Bobby the most elemental tasks of eating, drinking, and swallowing. They even tried using a straw. Despite the months of research and her growing understanding of traumatic brain injuries, Lucia questioned the state of her son's brain at this stage. Each day, he was visited by one kind of therapist or another, all of whom went patiently through the steps required to meet Bobby's most basic needs. Bobby struggled to do whatever was asked of him. His heart was willing, but his mind refused to cooperate. Most days ended in frustration for everyone. And yet, in determination they forged ahead every morning.

As hard as this was for Lucia, it was even harder for John—although, as usual, he did not vent his anxieties or desperation to his family or friends. He internalized his emotions, and it was only the dark shadows Lucia saw crossing his face that reminded her, again, that John had suffered through this sort of thing before. The realization of what her beloved husband was being forced to endure often reduced Lucia to tears.

It took Bobby more than a week to learn how to sip water from a straw. But he did learn. The HealthSouth Rehabilitation Hospital was well equipped to handle the specific needs of patients in Bobby's condition. It contained multiple rooms for therapy, depending on what was required. The physical therapy center in particular possessed state-of-the-art equipment and was staffed by trained and seasoned therapists. The experience of this talented staff gave Lucia and John immense comfort and hope, even with the daily disappointments and anxieties swirling around them.

Bobby, however, was not able to use any of these rooms. His therapy was confined to his own room because there he could use the private bathroom. His bathroom, too, was designed to accommodate a patient in Bobby's condition with minimum effort and inconvenience. In any case, Bobby was incapable yet of using any of the equipment in the therapy rooms.

At night, when everyone had left the room, Lucia tried her own brand of therapy.

"Bobby," she said. "Look at me. Look at my mouth and watch how the words come out. Can you do the same thing? Can you make any sound at all?"

No, he could not make a sound. He simply stared ahead with a blank look.

"Okay. Then let's try to eat something."

Each evening Lucia placed a tray on his lap with a bowl of warm soup on it. He showed not the least interest in eating any of it. Lucia knew from her research that Bobby had lost the memory of food. A king's feast could have been placed before him, or a dish of nondescript liquid, and he would not have known the difference, or cared. Only when his mother ate the soup herself and then rubbed her stomach with exaggerated delight did Bobby show, through his eye movements and tracking, a trace of interest in the food—or at least what his mother was doing with it. But when she followed up by slipping the spoon into Bobby's mouth, half of it would dribble out onto his napkin.

Lucia, however, chose to focus on the half that stayed in.

"Good job, Bobby! Isn't this soup yummy?" she would say. "It's cream soup, your favorite. Do you remember when you used to eat bowl after bowl of it? Can you say 'cream soup'? Here, let me give you a bit more. Would you like that?"

Success came in flickers. Several days into this routine Bobby gave his mother the slightest of nods, indicating that, yes, he would like a bit more.

"Good, Bobby!" she exclaimed the first time he did this. "Now, can you say the word 'soup'? I'll sound it out for you. Listen closely."

And she did sound out the word. Repeatedly. But to no avail. The encouraging words from the therapists could not counter Lucia's disappointment and frustration.

Her research continued despite the heavy demands on her time. She delved into any journals and books and periodicals she could lay her hands on. One thing she discovered, in an article written by a world-renowned neurologist, is that a patient coming out of a coma requires intense therapy and training immediately after regaining consciousness. If not, the consequences could be dire: bodily and mental functions lost temporarily as a result of the coma may be lost forever.

Lucia raised this issue during the weekly meeting with Bobby's caregivers.

"From what I've read in one of the clinical studies," she told them, "if functions lost by damage to the nerves have not come back within a year, they are less likely to come back at all. If they do, it will be because of the rewiring of the brain. To rewire your brain after a severe case of TBI, think of it as constructing a new road. If you put little effort into it, the new road won't be strong, and it will crumble and fade with time. However, if you put a lot of effort into it, you can formulate a strong, durable road that will stand the test of time. The same principle applies to rehab exercises. The more you practice and repeat an exercise, the stronger those new pathways in the brain become. Neuroplasticity is nothing without constant reinforcement and diligence."

Lucia then read aloud selections of that article.

"As you know" she said in conclusion, "Bobby was in a coma for three months. That doesn't give us much time. I realize we're all trying hard, but can we not expedite the process?"

The doctors and nurses and therapists looked askance at each other, but none offered an immediate comment, and the meeting adjourned with nothing concrete decided.

Nonetheless, what she had told the doctors became her mantra. She felt as though she held a ticking time bomb, and nothing that anyone could say consoled her or gave her renewed hope. John did what he could, both with words and actions, but at the end of the day he could do little to stop or even slow Lucia's continued slide into depression. She kept remembering Bobby the way he was—at barbecues with friends, on the football field, in the pool, swimming to his heart's content—and she yearned to once again see him thriving in his favorite settings.

The doctors offered little hope. Lucia understood why; the odds remained long for Bobby, and they didn't want to impart false hope. Although she continued to believe they sincerely cared for her family, they had to project a professional, standoffish demeanor, even when they expressed concern to Lucia for the state of her own health. She had lost more weight, and the dark circles under her eyes suggested that her insomnia was worse than ever. She looked exhausted. Utterly exhausted.

"Honey," John said one evening as he and Lucia sat on a bench in a hospital vestibule. "Do you remember our original goal? All we wanted—all we asked God for—was Bobby to wake up, to come out of his coma. Thanks to you, that is exactly what happened. Please don't get your hopes up. Think of what's been achieved. As it is, Bobby will be able to eat and drink and get around in his wheelchair. Eventually, he'll be able to speak well. What more do you want?"

Her man of few words had poured out his heart to her, and Lucia had to respond. "I want what you want, John," she said. "I want Bobby back with you and me and Peter. We can do this, you and me. We can do this. But we need to work fast."

"I understand," John said. "I understand you and I know how you'll go about this. That's exactly what worries me. If you push yourself too hard and you collapse, what good is that? Where does that leave us, beyond giving me another patient to attend to? Is that what you want?"

The look John gave her as he spoke would permit only one reply. It was the look of someone who had suffered too much in this life and did not want to endure further suffering.

"Okay," Lucia said. "I promise to take better care of myself, John, with your help. I'm sorry for the grief I've caused you and I'm sorry for not giving you the attention you deserve. I've been somewhat preoccupied in recent weeks," she added with a trace of a smile.

John nodded but did not smile.

This conversation then led to a discussion about whether to sell the chemical company. The couple had raised this possibility soon after the accident, but had ultimately decided to table it for the time being. Now, with the ongoing demands of a son in need and a company just getting on its feet, the time seemed right to Lucia to raise it again.

"I don't think we should," John cautioned. "You've worked so hard to make a go of it. You're one of the few female CEOs in this business, and consider how far you've come. Can you seriously envision handing the company over to someone else? I can't."

"Nor can I," Lucia confessed quietly.

"That company is our future," John went on. "It's our hope for the future. You and I both know that it has great potential.

But we can't base a selling price on potential, only on what's there now. So, we wouldn't get anything close to its real value."

Lucia once again appreciated her husband's wisdom and common sense, though she couldn't help but play devil's advocate.

"I appreciate what you're saying," she said, "but I can't help thinking that I'm splitting my precious time between the company and Bobby. I want to give Bobby my full attention."

"You are giving him your full attention, honey," John said. "No parent could give more than what you're already giving him. I would hate to see you give up on a company that you've built almost from scratch into something credible and admirable. Besides, if we sell the company now, we may have more capital and savings, but far less cash inflow. We need that cash inflow to pay all these medical expenses, not to mention Peter's college expenses. The money we'd get for selling the business would eventually run out."

They decided then and there not to sell the company. Lucia had always worked for what she had, from her earliest days as a freshman at the University of Kentucky to graduate school in London. Although she had been born into relative privilege, still she had fought hard for what she had achieved. It was simply her way, and she knew of no other. Her hard work had always paid off, and she was convinced it would continue to pay off—despite the doubts she was experiencing about her abilities, her resolve, and even God's love for her.

# CHAPTER 10

One night, Lucia made another suggestion related to finance and logistics: that they sell their house in West Lake Hills, an affluent area of Austin. The neighborhood contained some of the best public schools in Texas, which was the primary reason they had moved there. But now that both sons had left home, the Hurs no longer had a need for good schools.

"We'll get a good price for it," Lucia said as they lingered together over a bottle of wine in their kitchen, "and we can use some of the money to remodel the office building. We can open up the top floor and live there. More to the point, we can remodel it to accommodate Bobby and his wheelchair."

"And we'd cut down on commuting time each day," John added, reading his wife's mind. "That would give us more time to be with Bobby. And Peter, when he's able to come home."

"Exactly!" Lucia exclaimed. "You must be reading my mind, John!"

Thus, another important decision made.

For another month Bobby was trained in basic functions: eating with a spoon, drinking with a straw, brushing his teeth, sitting up, lying down. But because he could not learn to use the bathroom on his own, he had to rely on diapers. He was like a newborn baby stuck in the body of a full-grown adult.

With a normal brain, even a toddler can learn by holding experiences and memories securely in his or her mind and using these building blocks to master many tasks. Not so for someone suffering from a traumatic brain injury. He or she cannot remember those building blocks and must revert to step one whenever any task is put before them. Only by repeating the task over and over does the technique sink in and gain traction.

Once more Lucia found herself becoming exasperated. "Bobby," she would say, "you just learned how to do this. Can't you do it again? And can't you do it right?"

"Mrs. Hur," the therapist said on one occasion, "you should be thankful your son can understand you. If he couldn't understand you, no training of any kind would be possible. Can you imagine what that would be like?"

These words offered comfort to Lucia, and inspired a flashback: at the hospital in Lubbock, Lucia had often prayed to God to not take Bobby away. All she had wanted then was for Bobby to live. Now, Lucia was frustrated when he could not quite do what she wanted him to do. But at least Bobby was alive. He had not been taken away from her. And he was learning at his own pace and seemed keen to learn more.

With the use of his wheelchair Bobby was now able to visit the specially equipped rooms for treatment and training of brain-damaged patients, such as the physical therapy center and the speech therapy room. A favorite location for him was the pool on the third floor, a pool designed to treat patients in the water.

Bobby was put on a regimen that required a different training every thirty minutes. At its core were the three basics: physical, speech, and cognitive training. The speech therapist was working on teaching Bobby individual words. The therapist would say a word—car, for example—and ask Bobby to repeat the word. Bobby tried to comply but could not articulate any word. The sound he made was guttural in delivery, more like the sound an animal would make.

"He knows how to make the sound," the therapist noted at the conclusion of one session, when he noticed Lucia's disappointment. "It's a process; a slow one, to be sure, but a process nonetheless. We should be seeing some real progress soon."

*Maybe*, Lucia thought, although she was never one to sit back and wait and see. After John and the therapist left for the day, she became a trainer-in-training. She started talking to Bobby as though carrying on a normal conversation, not caring whether he understood what she was saying.

"How was your day, Bobby?" she might ask him. "Did you have fun? Did you learn a lot? How was your lunch? Are you hungry now? What if I got you a snack to tide you over until supper?"

She placed three of his favorite foods before him: melon, apple juice, and cream soup.

"Which of these would you like?" she asked him. She noticed him staring at the cream soup, but she ignored that. "Pick the one you want. I can't give you anything if I don't know what you want."

Bobby looked at his mother as though he was struggling either to understand what she had just said or to tell her what he wanted. He became agitated, but still the words would not come out, nor would his mother relent by offering him one or all of the choices.

"No, Bobby," she reminded him. "You will get nothing from me until you indicate what you want."

She disliked being so stern, but felt she had to be. Time was ticking away for any real hope of recovery.

"Oh, I see," she said to him. "You don't want any of these. I'll just take them away, then."

As she leaned over to pick up the tray, Bobby slowly raised his arm. It was a feeble but meaningful effort. To an outsider it would not have been at all clear what signal he was sending, but his meaning was clear to his mother.

"You want the cream soup, do you? Is that what you want?"

After what seemed an eternity, Bobby slowly, very slowly, nodded his head.

"Okay. We're making progress. Now, you have to use your spoon. You have learned how to use a spoon, haven't you?"

Lucia tied a bib around Bobby's neck and put a spoon in his hand. When Bobby made a haphazard stab at the bowl, the spoon fell out of his hand onto the bed. Lucia picked it up and put it back in his hand. Again, it fell out, and again Lucia put it back in his hand. She refused to help him eat. She just made sure the bowl didn't tip over, and she helped him aim his spoon. But otherwise she let him try and fail on his own. After repeated attempts, he was able to insert the spoon into his mouth and swallow.

"That's it, Bobby!" his mother encouraged. "That's how it's done. Good job!"

A normal person cannot begin to understand how difficult it is for a patient with traumatic brain injury to eat a spoonful of soup. After nearly an hour of disappointments, repeated stabs, and nearly imperceptible successes, Bobby managed to get half of the bowl into his stomach. The other half was all over the napkin and sheets, but that didn't matter. What he had achieved, he had achieved on his own!

Lucia knew people were saying things behind her back. She had overheard a team of nurses mumbling to themselves about what was transpiring in Bobby's room when Lucia began applying the cold towel to stimulate Bobby's senses. Some people had called her a woman of extraordinary willpower. Others had called her a tough bitch. It didn't matter what people said. Lucia knew what she had done then and what she was presently doing were the right things to do. Bobby had to relearn to perform these tasks for himself. He had to relearn to be independent. Otherwise, he would need to spend the rest of his life as a vegetable and in the hands of caregivers.

Bobby was also making some progress in speech therapy. His therapist, an affable man in his forties who seemed to have a personal stake in Bobby's recovery, had placed a poster on the wall exhibiting various body parts. This reminded Lucia of how she had placed posters of the human anatomy near the dinner table at home. If the boys had not learned anything new that day at school, they both had to learn and memorize various parts and organs of the body, or go without dinner. But now Bobby was relearning to associate these body parts as they corresponded with his own body. Each evening Lucia would review with Bobby what he had learned that day.

"Where are my eyes, Bobby?" she asked one evening. She placed his hand over her face. "Help me find my eyes."

Slowly, ever so slowly, Bobby moved his fingers to his mother's eyes.

"Good job!" Lucia exclaimed. "Thank you! You've earned a reward for doing that. What kind of cookies do you like?"

Lucia produced two different cookies and waited until Bobby stretched out his arm to take one of them. Because he was developing a healthy appetite, food was a good motivator, a good source of positive reinforcement, and an effective teaching tool.

Lucia realized that what she was doing may have seemed inhumane to some people, but she knew of no other way to proceed. Bobby's brain was a blank slate. He remembered nothing. Repetition was his only hope for rebuilding the memory banks in his brain.

Lucia looked forward to Sundays. Since it was her only day off work, she was able to spend larger, uninterrupted lumps of time with Bobby. It was during one of those days two months after Bobby had regained consciousness when she and Bobby were the only people in his room. John was at work and there was a skeleton crew on duty. Lucia sat next to Bobby's bed.

"What did you learn yesterday?" she asked him. "Tell you what: let's practice those words you learned."

Since awakening from the coma, Bobby had not opened his mouth to talk or utter a sound except when prompted. It was as though he had forgotten how to talk, which, in a real sense, he had.

She raised a glass of water and asked him what she was holding. No response.

She pointed at herself. "Who am I?" she asked earnestly. Again, she pointed at herself. "Bobby, who am I?"

No response.

Lucia let out a long sigh. She had done everything she could think of to get him to start talking, but nothing had worked. Looking away, she placed the glass of water on a table. As she did, she heard him say in a weak, flat monotone, "*M…o…m.*"

Lucia's jaw dropped. She felt a rush of powerful emotions.

"Bobby, did I hear you correctly? Can you repeat what you just said?" She brought his hands to her cheeks, now damp with hot tears. "Bobby, who am I?"

He looked at her. His mouth opened.

"M…o…m," he mumbled. His voice was weak, tentative, but audible.

It was a voice sent by the gods.

# CHAPTER 11

"Oh Bobby, Bobby," Lucia gushed, "that's right. You are so right." She swiped at her eyes with the sleeve of her blouse. "Yes, I am your mom!"

Just then, John arrived. Instantly he heard the sound of Lucia weeping and he saw the tears coursing down her cheeks.

"Honey, what's wrong?" he asked. "What happened?"

"Bobby said 'Mom,' John," Lucia managed. "He called me Mom."

John stood there, mute.

"Here, watch," Lucia said. She turned in her chair to once again face her son and put her hand on his. "Bobby, who am I?" she asked him. "Tell Daddy who I am."

"Mom," he answered, a bit more confidently.

John went to the other side of the bed and clasped his son's free hand. There they were, the three of them, a family bound together by the bonds of love.

"Yes, Bobby, she is your mom," he said. "No mom has loved her son more. She has worked so very hard to bring you out of your coma and bring you back to us."

From that moment, Bobby's speech improved both in quantity and quality of words. He listened intently to any conversation, whether it be between his parents or between his parents and the doctors, and struggled to sound the words out as he heard them. Often when he spoke words out of context that made no sense, people would laugh with him, blissful in the knowledge that every word spoken was another word potentially stored away in his brain for future use. Such was his progress that his doctors urged the Hurs to invite family and personal friends in to see him, to increase the breadth and depth of his vocabulary. Lucia and John immediately called just about everyone they knew to report the good news and to help spread the word about visiting the hospital.

As a result, the hospital set visiting hours for Bobby from one to three o'clock in the afternoons. The one stipulation was that all visitors were required to attend a brief session to orient them on Bobby's condition before actually visiting Bobby, else their shocked expressions upon seeing him might confuse or upset him. In addition, because Bobby's ability to digest sentences was limited, and his brain's processing time was delayed, only one person was allowed to speak with him, even when two visitors—the maximum allowed—were in the room.

On that first day of visitation, people started arriving at the hospital at noon. The hospital's intent was to host the orientation session in the cafeteria, but staff members quickly realized they would need to find a bigger room. By one o'clock, 180 people had gathered, just about everyone the Hur family knew well in Austin: neighbors, Bobby's friends, his parents' friends, teammates, and the like. Many of them had to be sent home and asked to return another day after the crowd had thinned. Bobby could meet with only two people at a time, and only for fifteen minutes each, the doctor told the visitors.

# BOBBY

Bobby and Lucia - Chair of
TACC - Gala

Bobby charming Mom
after a fight

Bobby learning to sit up

Bobby celebrating his first
walk without a wheelchair

Hur Chemical
Manufacturing Plant's
Christmas Party

Lucia and Bobby at the
Hur's Needy Gift Charity
Party in 2014

Lucia celebrating her birthday

# BOBBY'S GRADUATION

Bobby's graduation photo with brother Peter and his wife Steph

Bobby's graduation day with proud Mom and Dad

Bobby wheelchair days

Bobby's graduation ceremony at Texas Tech University.

# DREAM HOME BUILT BY JOHN FOR LUCIA

From kitchen overlooking pool

John & Lucia relaxing in family room

John Hur's Creation - dream home for Lucia

Renaissance Living Room

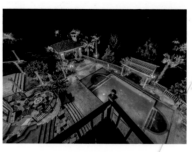

John's design of mosaic outdoor tile floor

Lucia's design of a perfect entry

Lucia in front of master entry before Fundraising Gala

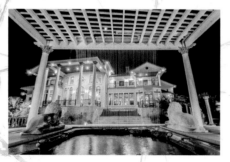

Lucia's spa tub

John's design of the back pool,
the perfect place to relax

Lucia's favorite place

# FAMILY CLAN

At Dad's funeral

Bobby and Peter on Cancun trip

The Choi-Hur family

Bobby and Peter in
middle school

Lucia's brother Augustine
wins the International
Amberson Award

Congressman Doggett and wife
Libby at John's 60th birthday party

Dad on his 80th birthday
with his four children

Dad's 80th birthday
reunion party

Dad and Thanksgiving

First family vacation after coma

Brother Francisco's new
house warming

Lucia and John start a new
life in Texas

Lucia and Sister Anna

Lucia and all Choi women
power!

Young Lucia with her
family in Singapore

Lucia and immediate family

Son Peter with wife Steph
at joint-birthday celebration

Bobby's welcome-home party
after hospital discharge

With Brother Dr. Augustine
and Dr. Mary Choi – Dean of
Weil Cornell Medicine

Dad with his kids at his birthday
celebration in Las Vegas

With Grandkids & Bobby

With brother Francisco
and sister Anna

His mind was like that of a baby, the doctor reminded them. But with their care and kindness, he said, Bobby could recover fairly quickly now, and go as far as the recovery process could take him—the extent of which was still unclear.

Everyone cooperated, and once again the Hurs' good friends Mike and Dee, Ed and Julie, Bob and Shirley, and Todd and Patti were there for them. Each couple took turns coming to the hospital to stand watch, allowing John and Lucia a couple of hours to get away by themselves.

These friends were Lucia and John's sounding board and helped them confront the manifold physical and emotional issues hounding them each day. The Hurs were blessed to have true friends looking out for them when the chips were down and they had no energy left, unable to cope with any more pain and sorrow. These special friends contributed more than their mere presence. They not only arranged Bobby's visiting schedule, they also divided the week's visitation time into certain blocks of weekdays and weekend days, with each couple assigned to be in charge of different parts of the week. In addition, they ensured that each visitor was advised to speak slowly and distinctly, and to introduce himself or herself as though meeting Bobby for the first time, but to then tell Bobby what their relationship had been before the accident. This was done in hopes of jogging Bobby's memory.

One of the first people to visit Bobby was Charles Kean, a friend and football teammate, and the one who had exchanged friendship rings with Bobby upon graduation. This was the ring Neil had recognized when Bobby was wheeled into the Lubbock hospital.

"Hi, Bobby," Charles said when greeting his friend. "I'm Charlie Kean. We played football together. Can I get a hug? Man, it's good to see you again. You're looking great!"

Bobby slowly wheeled his wheelchair over to where Charles was standing. Charles bent down and gave him a hug. The enthusiasm in his voice was infectious.

"Do you remember that game where we were losing by two touchdowns in the fourth quarter, but came back to win the game?" Charles said. "You were sensational, Bobby! You scored the winning touchdown with time running out. Man, did the crowd go wild. I can still hear them screaming your name!

"We were the best team in our league," he continued. "We almost won state. We couldn't have done that without you. You were the best. Do you remember playing football, Bobby?"

Bobby stared at Charles and slowly shook his head no.

"You were the best, Bobby!"

Charles gave Bobby the thumbs-up sign. Bobby tried to return the gesture, but could not. Lucia and John noticed the look of shock on Charles' face and hoped Bobby hadn't seen it. But they understood. To someone like Charles, it was nearly impossible to believe that the person sitting in the wheelchair was the same person who a year ago had fought off tacklers on his way to scoring yet another touchdown for his team. Charles kept a smile on his lips, as though he had witnessed nothing out of the ordinary, but his eyes expressed a depth of sorrow over the cruel twist that fate had played on his best friend.

Such meetings were having the desired effects, as Bobby seemed more and more motivated and stimulated. He appeared more inclined to want to accomplish something when visitors were around—far more than if only a parent or a therapist was in the room with him. When Bobby's former football coach came in for a visit, Bobby seemed particularly keen.

"Hey, Bobby!" the coach cried out. He had a physique to match his booming voice, and his grin brightened the room. "Wonderful to see you, son! Do you know who I am?"

Bobby shook his head no.

"Well, I'm pretty famous these days," the coach said. "I happen to be the one who molded you into one of the finest football players ever to come out of the great state of Texas. Mind you, I had a lot to work with. You were one hell of a player right from the get-go and a born leader. You deserve the fame, not me!"

For the first time since the accident, Bobby smiled. He may not have remembered what a coach did or what the game of football was all about, but Lucia sensed—and the therapist later confirmed—that Bobby reacted to the kindness and enthusiasm in the man's voice. His brain may have even pulled a memory or two from a distant, murky past.

"Bobby, I want to shake your hand," the coach said. "May I shake your hand?"

He reached out his hand to Bobby. John and Lucia and the therapist waited to see what Bobby would do. He knew what was being asked of him. The doctors and nurses would often ask Bobby to shake hands with them. Would he now respond to someone from the outside?

"Bobby," his mother urged, "the coach wants to shake your hand. He wants to congratulate you on your recovery."

Bobby nodded ever so slightly and held up his arm as if in slow motion. The coach took Bobby's hand in his and held it gently for several blissful moments. During that time, the smile never left Bobby's face.

"God bless you, son," the coach said with feeling. "I'll see you back on your feet soon, and I will always count you proudly as my friend."

He said his goodbyes and left the room, leaving everyone in it imbued with hope and courage.

Now that Bobby was back within his circle of friends, his training sessions went increasing well. Although he didn't always understand who was there and what was being said, the sounds of somehow familiar voices, mixed with laughter and good cheer, seemed to inspire him on to new heights. One activity he especially enjoyed was getting out of his room and exploring the hospital. In response to that interest, Lucia started using the term "going out" to either motivate or reward Bobby for activities well done.

"Bobby, if you go over there to turn out the light, we'll go out for a look around," she would say. "All you have to do is touch the lever and the lamp will turn off."

A simple task, but nonetheless a hard one for Bobby to execute. First, he had to get his wheelchair over to the lamp switch, a mere two feet away. The wheelchair was easy to operate. One button started the engine and another moved it forward, while two others allowed the operator to change direction. For Bobby, these simple tasks demanded his full attention and often brought frustration. He could not seem to remember which button to press for which purpose, and the muscles in his arm were so weak that the act of pressing any button posed challenges.

"Bobby, if you want to go out," Lucia would say to her son, "you have to operate the wheelchair. If you turn out the light, I'll open the door and we'll go out. Would you like that?"

Eventually, after considerable effort, Bobby would do what his mother had asked him to do. Everything was done in slow, delayed motions. When a command registered in Bobby's brain, the information had to be internally processed before he could react in any meaningful way.

Every day, Bobby faced a full schedule of learning and relearning words, studying body parts, memorizing the names of objects, and practicing eating and drinking and speaking. It was grueling work, without long breaks, but Bobby did not seem to mind. He kept at it, as tenacious as a bulldog in spirit but as weak as a newborn kitten in execution. John worried about his son's level of fatigue, but Bobby knew of no way to manifest exhaustion.

Time marched on with little improvement; the days were measured in small victories. Bobby's diet shifted from Ensure to soup to more solid foods. As it did so, his arm and leg strength increased. His speech also improved. Whereas before it was, "Mom, water," now it was, "I want water, Mom." To a layman's ear the difference was minimal. To a mother's ear, it was significant.

John noticed it, too, of course.

"Bobby asked for something yummy to eat today," he told his wife when she joined them mid-afternoon one day. John was smiling broadly. "He actually used those words."

"That's our Bobby," Lucia said with pride.

Lucia and John had once struggled to get through a day without breaking down. Now, with his improvement in speech and with his learning starting to take hold, a new universe opened for them. Bobby became chatty and more interested in almost everything and everyone. For the first time in many months, John and Lucia experienced genuine joy. It was glorious for them. Despite all they had experienced and all that they realized they still had to endure, they felt optimistic that Bobby would recover and live a fruitful life.

At least, that's how it seemed at the time.

# CHAPTER 12

As Bobby's faculties improved, more friends came to visit him, some for the third or fourth time. He was beginning to remember their names, although he still became confused and forgetful. His friends usually talked about old times: what they had done together on weekend evenings, the pranks they pulled behind their parents' backs. Bobby laughed along with them, but his parents weren't sure if he was reliving the memories or if he even understood what was being said.

"Do you remember the picnic we had with the girls on that camping trip?" a friend named Brandon asked. He gave Bobby a wink. "We had some fun out there, didn't we?"

A young man named Jim said, "Or how about the time we drank your parents' liquor and we filled the empty bottles with tea to cover our trail. When your mom found out what we did, man, did she get mad! I'll bet Coach never saw you run that fast on the football field!"

On that afternoon, after his friends had left, Bobby said with a smile, "I like...friends."

"I know you do, Bobby," Lucia said. "And they really like you. They are good people. They bring good memories, don't they?"

Bobby nodded.

Each morning, John and Lucia woke up wondering what new words and experiences Bobby would add that day to the deepening pool of hope. One afternoon, when they were sharing a pot of coffee in the hospital cafeteria with one of Bobby's doctors, Lucia asked, "When do you think Bobby will be ready to return to school?"

The doctor at first looked surprised. He then gave Lucia a brief smile.

"You're kidding me, right?" he said. "I've never known a patient who has emerged from a deep coma and gone back to school with any degree of success."

"You have known *none*?" Lucia pressed.

"Oh, a number of them have tried, but without success. Eventually they get too frustrated to continue."

"What happens to them then?" John asked.

The doctor shrugged. "That depends on the patient. Some take on a menial job; others try to learn a trade. The point is, at this stage of recovery parents have to be realistic. Consider what has already been accomplished and be content with that. I don't want to see you disappointed."

Lucia folded her arms on the table and leaned forward.

"Do you think Bobby could be the first successful case?" she asked.

The doctor returned her stare.

"Well, I can assure you that everyone in this hospital wants to see another miracle," he replied.

Lucia knew that the doctor meant well and was giving her advice based on statistics. And yet, what he had told her made her angry and sad at the same time. Lucia took comfort in the knowledge that this doctor was not Bobby's primary physician. He did not know Bobby, not really. He might know him as a patient, but he didn't know him as a person. For certain he didn't know him as well as his mother did. Bobby had always met challenges head-on. His teachers and football coach had called him tenacious. Whenever Lucia heard that word used in reference to her son, she had to smile. *They don't know the half of it*, she often thought to herself.

Would it be a miracle if he recovered sufficiently to go to college? Perhaps. But it would also be what Lucia expected of him. More to the point, it would be what Bobby expected of himself.

Early one evening, Lucia and Bobby were on their way to the cafeteria to enjoy a snack. Bobby had put in a full day, and Lucia felt he deserved a reward. But not until he had completed all the tasks necessary to get that reward.

She guided the wheelchair into an elevator specially designed to accommodate patients like Bobby.

"Press number one, Bobby," his mother said. "If you push number one, we'll go down to the first floor. That's where the cafeteria is and where your snack is. You can have whatever you want, but first you have to get us there."

Bobby maneuvered his wheelchair as best he could, but it took a while in the confined space. Lucia refused to help him despite the pleading looks he gave her and despite his stomach rumbling in protest.

"No, Bobby," she kept telling him. "You've done it before and you can do it again."

Finally, after considerable exertion, Bobby was able to press the correct number and the elevator started down. Several minutes later, they entered the cafeteria.

"Here's your tray, spoon, and fork," Lucia said after they had selected a table.

She was trying to teach her son to identify the correct utensil, and also how to eat ice cream and cake with a fork and spoon. It was a grueling process. Bobby dropped his fork several times, and it took some time for him to retrieve it off his tray. By the time he got to his ice cream, it had turned into a lumpy liquid. Predictably, much of the liquid ended up on Bobby's napkin and shirt.

On the occasional weekend, Peter would come down from Lubbock to visit his family. Bobby was glad to see him, and vice versa, but such visits were also trying on the boys' parents. Lucia didn't have much time to spend with her second son, which was difficult for her, since she sensed Peter's frustration. He was also concerned about his mother's health.

"Mom, you don't look so good," he said once. "You look tired. You need to take better care of yourself and you need to devote more time to Dad. He and I are part of the family, too, in case you've forgotten."

"I haven't forgotten, Peter," Lucia said. "And I'm sorry if you feel I've neglected you. At the moment, I have to give Bobby every minute I can. Dad is okay and so am I. Don't worry about us. Just do whatever you can for your brother. He's the one who needs your love and attention, just as he needs mine and Dad's, now more than ever."

In years past there had been tension between Peter and Bobby. For many years the two brothers were very close and did everything together. But when Bobby turned fifteen, he became more independent. He had his own circle of friends and his own football team; Peter spent more time volunteering as a fireman and paramedic. The two brothers remained close, but not like in earlier years. That fact saddened Lucia, then and now. She believed that Peter could be doing more to accommodate Bobby and help him along. Peter was trying, but given the logistics involved, it was not easy.

With Bobby now enrolled in various treatment and educational programs, the next step was to teach him how to write. Although he was beginning to express himself in spoken words, and found it uplifting, writing was extremely difficult. He could barely hold a pen in his hand and he could not draw a single line. It seemed as though his brain had no idea how to write, which was alarming. Writing would not only enable Bobby to remember words, it would also help his hand strength and coordination. There was no time to lose.

"Bobby," his mother said. "You like your brother, Peter, right? Can you write him a letter? He would enjoy that a lot."

Bobby nodded. He gripped his pen awkwardly and tried to write. But he could not. The pen fell out of his hand.

John was there, standing beside a therapist and watching. He looked worried.

"Bobby doesn't have the strength to do this yet," he said. "Aren't you pushing him a bit too hard? Shouldn't we slow down a little?"

Lucia had heard this line of reasoning before, from too many people. *We can't slow down*, she wanted to scream. *We don't have time for that.* Instead she said, "Nothing will happen, John, without practice. Lots and lots of practice."

"Your wife is right about that," the therapist said. "Nothing can happen without practice."

Lucia nodded at the therapist. She had a lot of respect for this man. It took ten days for Bobby to complete a reasonable facsimile of a circle, and when he did that, it seemed to pique his curiosity. He seemed eager to learn more, and the process was accelerated.

Lucia picked up the pen, put it back in Bobby's hand, and the practice continued.

A month later, when Lucia walked into Bobby's room, he handed her a piece of paper. "What's this?" she asked her son.

He pointed at the paper. She looked down at it and saw the word "Mom." It was the handwriting of a kindergarten boy, but that didn't matter. Lucia was pleasantly surprised.

"Did you write this? On your own?"

Bobby slowly nodded.

"Oh my." She hugged her son. "Thank you, Bobby. Thank you so very much. Do you think you could show me how you wrote this word?"

Lucia placed the pen and paper before her son. He bit his lower lip and gave the exercise his full concentration. It went slowly, a piece of a letter added to another piece of a letter, but after thirty grueling minutes he had written the word "Mom." He read it out loud to his mother.

"Well done, Bobby!" she said. "You did it. You wrote the word. There's no stopping our Bobby now. There's nothing you can't do!"

She gave her son a hug. A few days later Bobby handed her a postcard with the name "Peter" written on it. Lucia completed the name and address and wrote a few lines to tell Peter that Bobby had finally finished writing the name "Peter" on the postcard. This routine of postcard mailers continued weekly for months. It made Bobby happy, and it made Peter feel as though he was contributing to his brother's recovery.

Now that Bobby could speak, write, and get around in his wheelchair, Lucia wanted to try more challenging tasks. She constantly felt the pressure of time. The fact that five months had already passed since he came out of his coma made her anxious. There was so much more to accomplish and so little time to do it.

To properly rewire his brain and allow proper time for recovery, Bobby would have to cram in as much relearning as possible in the limited time remaining.

As had been true for months, Lucia's days were filled with Bobby and his learning. Even the clothes she wore played a key role. On one day she would wear a red dress, to show Bobby and teach him the word "red" and the color associated with it. The next day she would wear a blue dress, and the next day a yellow one. Each day was blessed with new things Bobby did or learned, and Lucia began to believe that one day she might be free of fear, worry, and despair. Not too long ago, she dreaded to get up in the morning.

Every night, after the therapists left for the day, Lucia took over the job of teaching Bobby. Bobby, in turn, seemed tireless on most days. The work of learning seemed more a pleasure to him than a burden; a salve to ease the pain.

"Let's go, Bobby," Lucia said to him one afternoon. "I'll help you into your wheelchair."

Bobby shook his head, scowled, and pursed his lips, reflexive signs that he didn't want to do anything or go anywhere. They were also indications that he wasn't all that pleased to see his mother. It had been a typically long day of training, and today he did seem tired. He indicated he just wanted to rest. His mother was insistent, however.

They went out into the vestibule and headed for the elevator.

"We're heading for the parking garage," Lucia said. "Let's see if my car is still there."

At the car, when Lucia put her arm around her son and tried to lift him up, Bobby pushed her arm away. He refused to budge. Lucia could not force the issue. Since Bobby was so much bigger than she, Lucia had to talk Bobby into doing whatever she wanted him to do.

"I know you're tired, honey," she said. "I'm tired, too. But if we don't do anything, you'll never get out of your wheelchair, or even out of your bed. You'll never know the world that's out there and all the pleasures and promises it holds.

"You're my son, Bobby," she added, gazing into his eyes. "I love you. I would never do anything to intentionally hurt you. I just want the best for you. But we have to fight, together, to achieve what we want to achieve and be the best we can be."

Bobby sat there, looking at her.

"Don't you want to be free of this wheelchair? Don't you want to walk outside and see the trees and grass and fields? Don't you want to see your friends, wherever they may be?"

Bobby slowly nodded.

"Well, you can do all those things. But to do them, we have to practice hard every day. There's no other way. The alternative is to sit and look out the window all day for the rest of your life."

It was a gamble, but not a wild throw of the dice. Lucia knew her son. She knew he had a soft and gentle side that she could appeal to, as she had done many times before. And she knew how much he hated being confined to a wheelchair. It took a moment, but at length Bobby reached out his arm to her and indicated he wanted to be helped up. He was, and mother and son enjoyed a ride together onto the streets of the city and into a park dotted with trees and ponds and playgrounds. Bobby loved it.

As Bobby's physical and psychological condition improved, so did his memory. Slowly but surely, he began recalling people and events in his life. The problem, however, was that his memories were out of sequence. They were like pieces of a puzzle that did not fit together. This lack of understanding of past and present tense confused the doctors as much as its effects confused Bobby.

On one occasion he remembered where his family had once lived in Austin. This recall surprised his mother.

"Bobby," she said, "you remember our old address?" She was impressed, and thought this memory of a long-ago address was a breakthrough.

But there was a downside to it.

Several days later, Lucia received a call from the hospital: the hospital administrator wanted to see her and John right away. No reason was offered, and this puzzled Lucia. The day before had been their weekly meeting with the medical staff, and nothing had been mentioned then. But she had to go, and she had to go alone. John was away, remodeling their new home, a task that had demanded much of his time in recent months.

When she arrived at the hospital, she went straight to the administrator's office, where the administrator handed over a piece of paper with some numbers written on it.

"Do you recognize that telephone number?" he asked.

Lucia looked down at the paper.

"Yes, I believe I do. That was our first phone number after we moved here to Austin." She glanced up. "How did you come by this number? And why are you telling me this?"

The administrator leaned forward against his desk. "It seems that your son has been calling this number early in the morning and asking to speak with his mother. The current owner of this number is none too pleased, and has been complaining. Rather loudly, I might add."

Lucia was so stunned she could not speak.

"Mrs. Hur?" the administrator asked. "Are you all right?"

Lucia shook her head. "I'm fine, thank you. I'm just surprised Bobby can remember that number. We had it so long ago. I'm even more surprised that he's calling it."

"Yes, well, first things first. The people Bobby has been calling want to talk with you. So, please give them a call."

On her way to Bobby's room, Lucia felt conflicted. Part of her was upset that Bobby was unwittingly harassing strangers, but another part of her was encouraged. To think that he could remember a phone number from the past and then call it! The recipient of the call had tracked down who was calling him, and Lucia understood why he was angry. But if he only knew what was involved here!

She went to Bobby's room to place the call, identified herself as the mother of the caller, and apologized. She tried to explain what had happened, and the man seemed sympathetic. But he explained that Bobby was calling early in the morning and waking up his family. "This must not continue," the man stated emphatically.

"May I please ask if my son said anything else, beyond asking for his mother?" Lucia said.

"I've had a hard time understanding him," the man said. "All I know for sure is that he keeps asking to speak to his mom."

"I see. Thank you. It will not happen again. If it does, call me, not the hospital administrator." She gave the man her number.

After she hung up, she asked Bobby for their home phone number. Without hesitation he gave her their old number.

"Bobby, that's not our number anymore," Lucia told him. "We changed our phone number after you boys left home. That number belongs to someone else now. You can't call that number again. You mustn't. Do you understand?"

Although Bobby sat there motionless, his eyes seemed to register her request.

Lucia took out a piece of paper and wrote down their current number. She read it aloud several times and asked Bobby to memorize it. After several minutes of silence, she again asked him for the number.

After several moments, Bobby recited the old number. After repeating this exercise several times, Lucia was on the verge of losing her temper, something she had promised herself she would never do.

"No!" she cried out. "That is not our number. *This* is our number," she said, shaking the piece of paper and holding it up in front of him. "You must *never* call the other number again. Not ever. Do you understand?"

Bobby cringed, but managed to nod. Nonetheless, he called the old number the next morning, and again the morning after that.

"Will you *please* find a way to stop these calls," the man said in no uncertain terms. "We are sick and tired of them. One more call from your son and we are calling the police."

Lucia apologized once more and asked the hospital to block the number from the phone in his room. That ended the calls. But when Lucia asked her son why he kept calling the old number and asking for his mother, Bobby did not reply.

Soon after this incident, Lucia and John noticed a shift in their son's behavior. His friends were still coming to visit him, and he still seemed to enjoy their company and conversation. But when they left, he turned cranky.

This crankiness then seeped into other areas of his daily routine.

For several weeks, Bobby and his mother worked on naming places—cities and states, for example—before he ate his supper. It was meant to expand Bobby's horizons, while also having fun, and with the extra motivation of good food. Their primary prop was a map of the United States.

"This is Colorado," Lucia might say, pointing at the Rocky Mountain State on the map. "You love Colorado. You spent several happy summers there counseling at a Christian summer camp. And this is where Peter lives in Lubbock. And this is Austin, where you, Daddy, and I live, and where we are now."

One evening, as they were starting out, Bobby pushed the unfolded map away.

"I don't want to do it!" he screamed at his mother. "You can't make me. Leave me alone!"

Lucia was shocked. Rarely had she heard her son sound so angry, certainly not since coming out of his coma. His pronunciation was awkward, but he had no trouble getting his point across.

"Bobby, what's wrong? Why are you doing this? Are you tired?"

Lucia tried to calm her son and figure out what was behind this erratic behavior. The doctors had told her and John that helping Bobby learn to express emotions such as shame and anger and pride would stimulate him to get better. So again, as with the early-morning telephone calls, this incident was both positive and negative: Bobby expressed an emotion—a good thing—but seemed irate with his mother and the world—a bad thing. Lucia wanted to cry. Instead, she steeled herself.

Lucia reached down to pick up the map off the floor. As she did so, Bobby threw the pen at her. She saw it coming and turned her head; the pen smacked her on the cheek. It hurt, but what hurt far more was the foul name Bobby called her. Clearly, Bobby was angry, and there was no reasoning with him. Not at this moment. Lucia left the room and walked swiftly to the parking garage. There she got in her car and wept uncontrollably.

She wept not because Bobby did not recognize how much she loved him and how much she had tried to help him recover. She wept for the loss of the child she had once known and loved so dearly, for the boy and then the young man he had been before the accident.

# CHAPTER 13

Bobby was playing organized football by the age of twelve. For the next six years, John and Lucia rarely missed a game, but it was the first game that Lucia recalled the best. The players in the backfield wore towels around their waist to help keep their hands dry so the ball would not slip out. Bobby, a halfback, had written on his towel, "I love Mom."

Lucia thought about this often. It had made her so happy, so proud.

After games, Bobby always said something nice to his mother. "Mom, you were the prettiest woman in the stands," he would say, or, "Mom, all the guys think you're great and so do I."

There was a catch, however. Most of the mothers in the neighborhood did not work, but Lucia did. Bobby did not tell his friends that she ran a chemical company, and he let it be known to Lucia that he wanted her to quit and stay home with her sons. Lucia being Lucia, she did tell Bobby's friends what she did for work, but always made sure, when she had to go to the office, that there was adult supervision and plenty for everyone to eat. John was also working at the time, and although he was riding the crest of a wave, he pitched in to help whenever he could.

When John and Lucia got married and Lucia was suddenly a mother to John's two boys, she was instantly anxious about juggling John, the kids, and her career. Due to the trauma of the death of their biological mother, Lucia wanted to shower these kids with love, trust, and understanding, and she developed a fierce commitment to ease their pain.

John left decisions regarding the boys' education largely to his wife, and Lucia wanted her sons to be raised in the way her father had raised her. She wanted to teach them how to serve, how to work hard for everything they wanted, and how to be independent. The boys were given an allowance in return for work around the house, and they were taught how to save money. Every month, the family reviewed their utility bill and discussed ways to use less electricity. The savings were minor, but the exercise, Lucia believed, was important.

In all they did, John and Lucia tried to serve as role models for their children. They wanted their sons to see how their parents interacted with each other and how they handled both joyous and stressful situations. Rarely did Susan enter the equation. Whatever influence she once had over her children had largely dissipated. Often it was Lucia who spoke of her and who tried to keep her memory alive.

"Do you remember your biological mother?" Lucia asked Peter and Bobby one day. "Her name was Susan."

They shook their heads, said the memory of her was vague, and went on with what they were doing. Lucia understood, and so did John. Their sons had been only three and four at the time of the accident, and although Susan had lived another three years, it was a life confined to hospital beds and doctors' appointments, without much interaction with her sons. John missed her, of course, and often felt sad that she had not been able to enjoy her life after working so hard to support her family. And he was sad that she never had the opportunity to say a proper goodbye to her children.

But all of that was in the past, and John was content to leave it there. Peter and Bobby never thought of Lucia as their stepmom. She was their mother. And since they were sometimes afraid of their father, they were more inclined to open up to their mother. Even though she demanded more of them than their father, and had more disagreements with them, the communication was better.

Those early years of marriage and football and dreams of the future were good years, and the memories of them both soothed Lucia and saddened her. Life was far different today.

Bobby had just thrown a pen at her, which hurt her both physically and emotionally. But she would not cry anywhere but in the car. It was the only place she could be alone to express her feelings. John was often at home; Bobby and the medical staff were at the hospital; and her employees were at the office. There was nowhere else. She could not go to her close friends, as that would mean incurring an additional burden, and they were already doing more than enough for the Hurs.

One time, not long ago, Bobby had inadvertently done something to upset Lucia, and she had driven home and was crying in the kitchen when John came home. Immediately, she retreated to a closet. She didn't want her husband to see her crying. John finally discovered his wife's hideaway—he had seen her car in the driveway and heard her sniffling—and coaxed her out.

"If you want to cry," he told her softly, "why do it in a dark closet? Do you think I would somehow think ill of you?"

"Yes," Lucia said.

"Well, you're wrong. I could never think ill of you." He hugged his wife and gently massaged her back until the tears dried. It was a moment she would never forget. Still, she resolved never to let John see her cry again. She also decided not to tell him things that would upset him. What had happened today, for example. Doing so would only make him mad and would solve nothing.

As she drove home from the hospital that evening, Lucia was reminded of what her mother used to say: "There is an old cliché that says your personality determines your fate. This fits you perfectly, Lucia. Your personality is making your life harder and harder. You are an idealist and a perfectionist."

At the time, Lucia did not pay much attention to this. She assumed her mom had said it because she disapproved of Lucia's decisions involving John and the boys. But now, as she drove along the streets of Austin, she sensed that her mother had known something Lucia did not. At times like this, she missed her mom. It would be bliss beyond belief, she thought once again, to have her mom here with her. She could use her sage counsel and valuable insights about life, love and labor.

At a young age, Lucia had learned to handle the inevitable stresses of life on her own, and never came to rely on her parents or on anyone else to provide moral or emotional support. Whenever necessary, she retreated within herself to find her own way of solving whatever issues needed to be solved.

While in the end it all worked, Lucia had not always admired her mother. When her parents came to America, her once-famous father, Dr. Youngsoo Choi, renowned as Asia's first cardiovascular surgeon to perform a successful open-heart surgery, worked long hours to support his family. Her mother, a professional dancer in her younger days and now a homemaker, seemed interested only in taking care of herself and Lucia's youngest sister, Anna. She made it clear that she, and she alone, would make Anna's dreams of becoming a world-class violinist come true. Her days were consumed with shopping and with visits to spas, hair salons, massage parlors, and nail shops, in addition to managing Anna's musical career.

Lucia's mother admired her husband for urging their children to enter the sciences. She wanted to contribute as well, but various undiagnosed health issues prevented it. She often stayed in bed complaining about one ailment or another.

Whenever she needed to go someplace important, such as a hospital or an attorney's office, she took Lucia to act as a translator.

Lucia urged her mother to learn English, but her mother claimed she was too old to pick up a new language. Lucia's father was not much help. He worked grueling hours and had precious little time for such matters. Lucia's brother Francisco, the first-born, was no help at all: he did not get along with their father and alienated himself from the rest of the family. Lucia's two younger siblings, Anna and Augustine, were too young to contribute much. Thus, the burden of responsibility and home management fell to Lucia.

Lucia's father was a thirty-four-year-old lieutenant in the Korean army when he performed his first open-heart surgery. It was a great success, and his future seemed bright. But he decided to leave his homeland because he opposed the military government and its dictatorial policies. At the time, the government of Malaysia was interested in learning the techniques of open-heart surgery. Dr. Choi was invited to go to Malaysia with his family to practice his craft and to train other doctors. He found the invitation appealing for a variety of reasons, not the least of which was that English was an official language, since Malaysia was then under the British sphere of influence. Dr. Choi planned to emigrate to the United States, where opportunities abounded, but first he wanted his children to speak English. Plus, he wanted to save some money before coming to the States.

At the age of eight, Lucia moved with her family from Korea to Malaysia. She was placed in a Catholic convent school run by Irish nuns, who were strict in both their teaching methodologies and their dispensing of discipline. Her father also made Lucia and her siblings work hard in their studies, with English being his primary focus.

Nevertheless, life in Malaysia was good. Dr. Choi was making good money and the government was otherwise catering to the family's needs. They were able to hire several maids, which freed Lucia's mother to pursue a life of socializing and shopping. The care of the children fell to the maids, which made Lucia question her mother's love for her.

When Lucia was nine, Malaysia was hit by a terrible tropical storm. The wind, rain, thunder, and lightning were horrific. Despite the weather, Lucia believed she still needed to attend the weekly crusade meeting at the church, which was spearheaded by a jovial Irish nun who would later influence Lucia's spiritual growth. So, Lucia set out on her own, walking to the church through a torrential rain, and she arrived at the appointed hour, met by a nun who was clearly stunned to see one of her young pupils standing before her, completely drenched. She took Lucia in her arms, and as she was talking gently to her, a car pulled up outside. Together they glanced out a window to see Lucia's mother hurrying out of a cab. When she burst through the front door and saw her daughter safe and sound with the nun, she dropped to her knees and wept. When Lucia went over, her mother clasped her with a ferocious intensity and wailed even louder. It was a seminal moment for them both. Lucia never again doubted her mother's love.

As the years rolled on, Lucia learned more and more from her mother, not only insights into household duties and management—which largely remained with Lucia—but insights into the human heart and mind, and the world at large.

Such was Bobby's heritage, and it was a good one. His grandfather, his uncles, and his aunts all achieved the American dream, mostly in medicine, economics, and the sciences. Anna was a notable exception: after graduating from Juilliard with both a bachelor's and master's degree, she became the world's youngest female concertmaster and worked at the prestigious Teatro San Carlo in Naples, Italy. Even Lucia's older brother, Francisco, finally pursued his own dream and became a renowned architect. He worked with I. M. Pei & Partners and Kohn Pedersen Fox Associates, the world's most elite architectural firms.

The only one of the children who followed their father's footsteps was the middle child, who became Dr. Augustine Choi. At the time of their father's death, Augustine was the chairman of Weill Cornell Medicine. He eventually became the dean.

Sadly, Lucia's dad did not live long enough to see the fruits of all of the personal sacrifices he had made in pursuit of a better life for his children.

Underlying this family history was the love and respect each had for the other, growing only stronger as the years rolled by and elder family members passed on. That love and respect set a fine example for the boys, and it is part of what gave Lucia and John and Bobby and Peter the strength to continue on their journey toward recovery for Bobby.

They still had a long way to go, and the pathway to deliverance remained fraught with potholes.

# CHAPTER 14

By now Bobby's speech had improved to the point where he could carry on a conversation. His pronunciation was far from flawless, but most people could understand what he was saying. And while his speech and inflection improved, so did the strength in his arms. Because he was now able to operate his wheelchair on his own, he was flirting with a degree of independence.

As his doctors became more cautiously optimistic, Lucia became ever more insistent on pushing her son as hard as prudence dictated. Her philosophy was that she should always try her best to achieve and to serve, and this dictum ruled every facet of her life, from school to her professional career to her role as a mother. She hoped that by setting an example, she could pass her approach to life on to her two sons.

The time bomb continued to tick. In Lucia's mind, the road to TBI recovery was dictated by the amount of time the brain took to reconnect all the broken chains, to recreate new wiring for the brain. She was constantly reminded that whatever abilities Bobby did not relearn within the next few months, he was likely to lose forever. So she pushed him ever harder, and that push instigated another heart-wrenching incident.

Bobby was no longer receiving therapy of any kind in his room. Instead, he attended sessions in his wheelchair. The most grueling part of the day was physical therapy. One exercise involved him sitting on a bench and giving high-fives to staff members, while at least one other person stood by to ensure he did not fall. The purpose was to teach balance while lifting his arms. The process was repeated over and over again, usually with mixed results. After that, he would be placed back in the wheelchair and coaxed to lift one leg and then the other, over and over again.

It was hard work. Bobby was a hefty young man who required a hefty therapist to help lift him and turn him. John often pitched in, and when he did, he was soaked in sweat by the time the session was finished. By now, the entire medical staff and the other patients on the floor knew Bobby. As group exercises grew more challenging, Bobby's competitive spirit shone through and he strove to outdo the other patients. He was rarely able to, however. He was the most handicapped patient in the room, and while his mind wanted to excel in front of his fellow patients, his body would not permit it.

Lucia walked into Bobby's room one afternoon to find her son and his father both looking exhausted. John gave her a long-understood signal that Bobby had had a hard day. Lucia signaled back that she understood the message. She then shifted her gaze to her son.

"Hello, Bobby," she said cheerily. "How did your day go today?"

Bobby's expression was as sour as his tone of voice. "I don't want to go to PT," he spat. "I want to practice alone."

"Bobby, listen to me," Lucia said. "You have what it takes to succeed in anything you set your mind to. You proved that in the classroom and you proved that on the football field. But to succeed you have to work hard and do what the doctors tell you to do. If you don't, you'll spend the rest of your life in the wheelchair or in bed. Is that what you want? To spend the rest of your life as a handicapped person unable to do much of anything? If it is, say so to your father and me right now. We won't force you to go to physical therapy anymore."

Bobby scowled but offered no further comment. After several suspenseful moments, he grudgingly began heading toward the physical therapy center. John went with him. Once there, he was transferred from his wheelchair onto a specially designed treadmill. Because he still could not maintain any balance when in an upright position, he was fitted with a special belt that secured his body in place. The therapist instructed him to walk, which he did, awkwardly. As strong and tough a man as John was, it was all he could do to avoid comforting his son in some fashion. Bobby was becoming increasingly frustrated by the seeming futility of it all—what progress he was making from week to week was in baby steps—and it was hard for John to just stand there and watch.

After her husband left for the day, Lucia, as was her wont at this stage of recovery, focused Bobby's attention on matters more mental than physical. Writing had long been a passion of Bobby's, and he once fancied himself quite the poet. His parents and his teachers were impressed by his abilities as a wordsmith, and now that her son's mental faculties were improving, Lucia sought to reignite his love of words. As always, however, the process was a challenging one, replete with properly placed motivations and even mild threats that she deemed heartbreaking but necessary. Bobby's brain was essentially a blank screen that had to be exercised not only to learn, but also to retain what he had learned.

"Bobby, here is a list of vocabulary words I want you to learn before dinner. Okay?"

Bobby stared blankly at the list of words.

"If you don't learn them," Lucia warned, "there will be no dinner for you."

She pointed to the tray of food resting on the bedside table.

When her son continued to glare at her, Lucia picked up a newspaper and began reading it. It was then that Bobby seized her wrist and twisted it, hard. A searing pain shot through her lower arm.

"Shit," he snarled at her, his eyes bright with fury, "you are not my mother. Why are you bothering me this way? Leave me alone!"

Lucia was stunned to her core. She couldn't believe what she had just heard. As Bobby had improved, especially in his speech, he had become more bellicose and resentful, which she could tolerate. She could even sympathize to a certain degree. But his latest outburst went too far.

"Stop treating me like a retarded baby!" Bobby added in that same demeaning tone of voice. "I'm tired of it!"

"Bobby," Lucia said, struggling to maintain her composure. "Why are you acting this way toward me? I don't deserve this. I am only trying to help you. I am only trying to help you remember the words you love so much. Do you remember how much you loved to write poetry?"

Bobby shook his head. "I can do it on my own. I can! I don't need you!"

Bobby turned on his side and lunged for the tray of food. As he did so, he lost his balance and rolled over onto the table and onto the floor, the food falling on top of him. Lucia tried to help him up, but he was too heavy. She ran out of the room, seeking help. Two nurses and an orderly came running and soon put things right.

Once she knew that Bobby was not hurt and had settled in with another tray of food, Lucia left the room. She wanted to be alone, to take a walk, to reflect. She also did not want her son to see his mother cry.

She walked outside and into a small park-like area adjacent to the hospital. Lucia had given up so much to be there for Bobby, to care for him as her son. Though Lucia had a lifelong dream of having a baby with John, that had not come to fruition.

She knew that if she had another child, she would be compromising the care she provided to Bobby and Peter. Though it was a painful decision, Lucia knew that she would have to sacrifice her dream to be the best mother to the children she had now.

Bobby had physically hurt her and had sent an arrow through her heart by saying she was not his mother. Yes, she understood his frustration. His training and therapy were getting harder as his vital signs improved, and he needed to vent his emotions on someone. Who better than his mother? Who else was there? Because the love a mother offers her child is unconditional, the child often uses her as a target, an excuse for his or her deficiencies.

The next day, Lucia asked Bobby's primary doctor for an assessment of her son's behavior.

"Mrs. Hur," the doctor said, "what your son is experiencing and what he is expressing is quite typical in this process. It indicates that his brain is emerging from a passive state. He is not really angry at you. He is likely angry at himself. He knows that he was once a good athlete who did everything well and who had lots of friends. Now he can't accept what he's become. Bobby can't take out his anger on this father because he's scared of him. Nor can he take it out on the medical staff here. So that leaves you. Like many patients who have survived a terrible accident, he blames his parents for letting him live rather than being grateful for being alive. It's a tough transition, but it will pass. The best thing you can do now is just be there for him. And hang in there."

When Lucia went home that evening, she was resolved to tell John nothing about the incident. It would have just made him upset. But when she walked into the kitchen, John took one look at her and said, "What happened to your wrist?"

Lucia glanced down. It had swelled even more during the drive home.

"I'm not sure," she said. "I must have sprained it lifting something heavy at work."

"Why are you lifting anything heavy at work?" John asked. "You have employees. Ask them to do it. That's what you pay them for."

Lucia nodded. "You're right, honey. I'll ask them to do that kind of work in the future. I promise."

"Right, then. Please see a doctor tomorrow and have it checked. I don't like how it looks."

Lucia did not like how it looked, either. Or felt. Her wrist throbbed with pain. Early the next morning she went to see her doctor. After a round of X-rays, the results showed a cracked bone in her wrist.

The doctor applied bandages and a small splint.

"You can still drive," he told her as he finished up, "but you won't be able to use your left hand for anything for a few months."

Lucia accepted the verdict, but was determined not to interrupt or even slow down her sessions with Bobby.

"You can hurt me, but you can't stop me," she said aloud on her way to work. "I will never give up on you."

A week later, several of Bobby's friends came to visit him. They were enjoying themselves, and when it came time for them to leave, Bobby said, "Mom, I'd like to say goodbye to my friends in the parking garage. Can I?"

What Bobby wanted his mother to do was help guide his wheelchair for him down to the garage.

"If you can operate your wheelchair by yourself down to the garage, you can do it," Lucia responded. "But I can't help you, because yesterday you did not finish your homework."

His friends already knew not to volunteer to help Bobby. As they rose to leave the room and go home, Bobby pointed at Lucia and said to them, "She is not my mother. She's mean to me. And she won't leave me alone!"

Bobby's friends looked at him and then at his mother, shocked. They clearly felt sorry for her. As calmly as she could manage, Lucia said to them, "It's okay, boys. Bobby sometimes says things like that when he doesn't get what he wants. He doesn't mean anything by it. Thank you for coming to see my son, and please come again soon."

The three boys left the room without saying a word. When the door was closed behind them, Bobby picked up a flowerpot and threw it at Lucia. She ducked out of the way.

"Bobby," she said, rising from her chair, "that kind of behavior is unacceptable. I won't have it. I can't take care of you any longer. From now on, Dad will be with you all day. I am going to tell him what you did, and he will make sure that you never do anything like that again. Do you understand?"

The threat of his father serving as his full-time caregiver calmed Bobby down. The notion clearly did not appeal to him.

He picked up the list of place names that he was supposed to have studied yesterday and without another word went to work.

"That's better," Lucia said, and sat down.

The next afternoon she asked him, "Bobby, do you like your wheelchair?" She already knew his answer.

"No!" Bobby replied with feeling. "I hate it!" He emphasized his point by pounding on the wheels with his fists.

"How can you hate something you live in?" Lucia said. "Do you want to live in this wheelchair the rest of your life?"

Bobby shook his head.

"Right, then," she said. "Here's what you have to do. The first thing you need to practice is using your wheelchair to the point where you don't need me or anyone else to help you. Then you have to practice standing up and walking. This will take a while, and I know you will get discouraged. You will fight me, your doctors, and therapists. But there is no other way. If you want to be independent and live a normal life, you have to practice, practice, and practice until you feel you can't possibly take another step. Then you have to get up and practice some more. Got it?"

Bobby nodded, but his heart was not in it.

"You can do this, Bobby," his mother pressed. "You can do this. You were a star athlete in high school. You have what it takes. It will be hard, but you can do it. You can walk out of this hospital with your head held high. This is what I want for you. This is what Dad wants for you. More than anything in this world. Do you hate us for wanting that?"

Bobby shook his head.

"You were in a terrible car accident. You were in a deep coma for months. It's a miracle you came out of it. And it's a miracle that you are able to work so well with the staff here. Everyone loves you. Everyone wants the best for you, especially Dad and me. You have no idea how many times I prayed to God to bring you back to me. I promised him that if he did, I would devote my life to helping people. That's one promise I intend to keep. Do you hate me for that?"

Bobby, who had been listening intently to what his mother was saying, shook his head.

"No, Mom," he said softly. "I don't hate you."

"I'm glad to hear that," Lucia said. She smiled at her son.

As the days passed, Bobby began trying to do more on his own. Getting from his bed into his wheelchair, and vice versa, was a particularly grueling exercise, but he was making good progress. He continued to be quiet and even resentful when his mother was with him, but Lucia rationalized her son's behavior by telling herself that Bobby was still sick and therefore was not yet himself, which was essentially what the doctors were telling her.

Still, despite her rationalizations, Lucia was confused and saddened by Bobby's attitude. She had never considered him a stepson, but she sensed that he considered her a stepmother, not his real mother. She feared that such a notion was deeply embedded in him and rose to the surface whenever he became angry. She wondered if Peter felt the same way about her. The thought always made her teary.

She knew that if John found out about Bobby's recent attitude toward her, he would be furious. For peace in the family she decided to keep everything to herself. Some nights, on her way home, she would cry. Other nights she would be excited by what progress she had seen at the hospital. If Bobby said something hurtful to her, she didn't go home. Instead, she went to the office and worked out her frustrations until the wee hours of the morning. She understood that such a rollercoaster ride of emotions was not healthy for her or John, but she saw no alternative.

# CHAPTER 15

A year had passed since the accident. In more recent months, Bobby had gone through several wheelchairs, since each one had been customized to his condition at the time. The one he had now was for more advanced patients who were able to get around on their own. Each step up made his parents happy, because each new wheelchair represented another step toward recovery.

Then there came the day when the physical therapist told Lucia and John that Bobby had graduated to the bar. He would no longer be on the treadmill with heavy straps around his waist to hold him in place. Instead, he would try to walk while clutching a bar at eye level. It was an exercise reserved for the most advanced patients.

"Way to go, Bobby!" John said when he heard the news. "Well done!"

"Congratulations, Bobby!" Lucia exclaimed.

"I should have started this sooner. He should have let me," Bobby said, gesturing to the therapist.

Lucia was unsure what her son meant, although she was pleased that he was clearly up to the challenge.

"I knew you could do it," she added. "You were a star football player. You have strong legs. Everyone cheered when you took the field."

Bobby smiled at that. Everyone in the room returned his smile.

The next morning, John took Bobby to the physical therapy center. What Bobby had to do was transfer himself from the wheelchair to a normal-looking chair, then hoist himself up and seize the bar with both hands. At first, the therapist resisted helping Bobby through the movements. Ultimately, he had to help him up while John stood by, watching helplessly.

Frustrations mounted when Bobby was in the chair and told to stand up and grab the bar. He tried but couldn't. His hands slipped off the bar and he slumped back onto the chair.

"You can do it, Bobby," his father exhorted. "You can do it. You're a strong boy. Use the muscles in your arms and hands."

Bobby tried again, but could not get up. A third and fourth attempt yielded the same result. John knew why. To do what he needed to do, Bobby needed strength in his abdomen and legs as well, and those muscles were not as well exercised as those in his arms. At length, the therapists stepped in and helped Bobby up.

"Can you move your feet?" the therapist asked him.

Bobby tried. He gritted his teeth and gave it all he had. His arms trembled and his body became soaked in sweat. He took one step forward and then fell back onto the chair.

"Well done!" the therapist said. "You took one step today. Tomorrow you'll take two steps, and three the next day. That's how it works."

John walked over and squeezed his son's shoulder.

The next day it took thirty minutes to get Bobby into the chair and then up to grasp the bar. He took one step and stopped. John tried to encourage him, but he could see the keen disappointment written on his son's face. He shook his head at the therapist. The session was over. Bobby could do no more.

That afternoon, John briefed Lucia on the day's activities. She kissed him goodbye and walked over to sit beside her son.

"Dad told me you took one step today," she said. "Good for you! Can you show me? I would love to see my son walk again!"

Bobby turned from her and went quiet. Lucia decided not to press the issue, lest her words trigger him. By now she not only understood his moods, she anticipated them.

Exercises on the bar continued for another six months. At the end of that period Bobby was able to walk the thirteen feet from one end of the bar to the other. The first time he did that, his parents gave him a rousing round of applause.

Of all the milestones Bobby had reached and passed since the accident, this was perhaps the most significant. What Lucia and John wanted desperately for their son was for him to be independent, a contributing member of society—to live a life with dreams fulfilled. Today, that vision, once so far over the horizon, now seemed within reach. Today, right before their eyes, as Bobby strove to put one foot in front of the other and walk, their own dream was being realized.

That first time, it took Bobby almost an hour to walk the thirteen feet. Each day after that, the time lessened until the process consumed thirty minutes, then twenty, then ten. The road was still not an easy one. Walking without the bar proved to be nearly impossible at first. He lost his balance and fell a number of times. But each time he forced himself back up, a stony look of determination upon his face. It was as though the fiery heroism he had displayed on the football field—and the gut-wrenching work and soul-demanding sacrifices it had taken to get to that point—had suddenly sprung loose from somewhere deep within his being to wash through his heart and up to his brain.

In the hallway outside Bobby's room, attached to the wall, was a long bar that patients in Bobby's condition could use. One evening after dinner, Lucia asked Bobby to walk along it and hold on with one hand. He did, and kept walking all the way to the elevator leading down to the parking garage. When he got out, he spotted a Suburban that looked like the Hurs' and tried to get in.

"What are you doing, Bobby?" Lucia asked him. "That's not our car."

"I want to go home," he said, his tone conveying a sense of urgency.

"Bobby, we can't go home now. But we can soon, if you keep practicing. You need to be independent when we do go home, because your father and I will not always be there with you."

Lucia had to all but drag her son back to his room. He did not want to go. He no longer wanted to return to what was; he wanted to venture forth toward what could be. But he did as his mother requested, and from then on, as a reward each time he did anything good, Lucia took him back down to the parking garage, where Bobby sat in his wheelchair watching the cars drive by toward the exit. Lucia's heart broke when he did this. He had been in this hospital for more than a year. And while he had showed vast improvements during that year, emotionally and mentally he was still the equivalent of an elementary school child.

"Keep practicing, Bobby," Lucia said on a daily basis. "Keep practicing. If you do, one day soon the doctor will say, 'Bobby, you can go home now.'"

In fact, Dr. Morledge said that very thing when Bobby completed his elementary school education.

"We no longer see any need to keep Bobby here at the hospital," he said. "No treatment we might recommend requires that. As we have already discussed, he can continue his rehab from home. In fact, you may see a marked improvement in his progress as a result, because he will be happy."

The Hurs greeted this long-anticipated announcement with silence. After a moment, John said, "Thank you, Doctor. This is a big decision for us. Please give us some time to think about it."

Lucia found John's response predictable. His pragmatic side almost always shone through. But in truth, she was not sure about the doctor's suggestion, either. Questions lingered. Her son had full days of rehab scheduled at the hospital. Could she and John do what Bobby's therapists had been doing all these months? Assuming they could, would their caregiving be anywhere near as good? Yes, they would be going to another hospital, St. David's Rehabilitation, for daily outpatient rehab services, but that facility was more than an hour's drive each way from their home. Could they effectively manage the logistics of such a schedule? Most importantly, could they keep him safe? Bobby continued to have problems with his balance. Given that, would he be prone to accidents when he tried to move from a chair to a sofa, for example? In the hospital there was a full-time staff to attend to him. What might happen at home if Lucia and John were gone from the house even for only a few minutes?

John and Lucia had discussed these questions at length in previous weeks and months. All that, however, had been theory. Now that the hour of decision had arrived, a cold reality settled over them both. Their home was ready to receive Bobby since it had been remodeled to make it as wheelchair-friendly as possible. Whether or not his parents were equally ready to receive him was another story.

Of course, both John and Lucia realized they would be simply delaying the inevitable by delaying the transfer. They could not keep Bobby in the hospital forever just for their own convenience. Among the most prominent reasons was the fact that the hospital could then make Bobby's room available for another urgent-care patient, one who may have suffered a similar kind of traumatic brain injury and needed the room far more than Bobby did now.

"Let's do it," Lucia said that evening over dinner. "We know we *can* do it. We've been doing all of that and a lot more in the hospital. I will take Bobby to rehab every day. You can take over after you come home from work."

"What about your company?" John said. "Will it suffer with you being away so much?"

"No. I'll just be switching my hours around a little, that's all. Besides, I have good employees now. All they need me to do is make major decisions, which I can still do."

John went silent, thinking. Then he said, "Okay. Let's do it."

The decision was made. After a year and five months at the hospital, Bobby was finally coming home.

# CHAPTER 16

A festive mood permeated the hospital the day Bobby left. Dressed and ready to go before breakfast, he was happier than anyone had seen him in a long time. It took a while for him to say goodbye, which he did by giving a high-five to every member of the hospital staff, each of whom congratulated him on his recovery to date and wished him well.

"Don't forget to continue practicing, Bobby," was a common exhortation. "There's still a lot of work ahead of you. But you can do it. Look how far you've come!"

Many of them said, "Come back and visit us."

"Don't worry, we'll be following your progress," Dr. Morledge said as he offered Bobby his hand. "You can't get away from us that easily!" He gave a slight squeeze. "It's because we care," he added in earnest. "Everyone here really cares about you."

They shared a smile before the doctor turned his attention to Bobby's parents.

"Congratulations, Lucia," he said, shaking her hand and then John's. "Because of your hard work and dedication, we have witnessed a miracle in this hospital."

"Thank you, Doctor," Lucia said with feeling. "It was teamwork that allowed this miracle to happen. Teamwork and God's blessings."

Buoyed by the warm congratulatory messages from the doctors and nurses, Lucia and John nonetheless heard unspoken words underlying them: *You are in charge now, Mr. and Mrs. Hur. We here have done all we can do. The rest is up to you. It will be very, very hard work, and we truly wish you the best of luck.*

Those unspoken words hung close to them as they waved their last goodbyes to the staff and guided their son's wheelchair down to the parking garage. They were on their own now. And Bobby still had so much to learn: how to dress himself, how to socialize, how to eat dinner in a dining room, how to take a shower, how to gain balance and walk without support, how to read at a more advanced level, how to talk coherently. Many of these activities had been introduced by therapists at the hospital. But these therapists were no longer in the picture. They were no longer an integral part of their lives. The Hurs were on their own.

As they approached their car in the garage, John and Lucia chanced a glance at each other. Each knew what the other was thinking without having to ask. Bobby, meanwhile, was humming to himself and tapping on the arms of his chair.

"Are you excited, Bobby?" his father asked him.

"I am," Bobby replied. "I'm very excited."

"Will you miss your friends here at the hospital?"

"Yes, I will. I will come back to see each one. But I am excited to go home."

A considerable group of friends had gathered at the Hur residence to welcome Bobby home. When John turned the car into the driveway, they all came over in greeting. When Bobby got out of the car, they broke into applause. Bobby looked puzzled as his gaze went from the small crowd to the building.

"Bobby," his father explained, "this is our new home. It was once the office building that Mom and I worked in. It still is. But we have remodeled the top floor for you. You'll see. You'll be able to get around in the house without much trouble."

Bobby gave everyone a quick wave and went inside with his parents. Lucia showed him his room, all of its amenities fashioned for her son's convenience. Basically, the entire top floor had been remodeled as a wide-open floor plan so that Bobby could move in and out of the rooms with his wheelchair.

"Do you like it?" Lucia asked tentatively.

Bobby gave no reply other than a slight nod of the head.

From day one it was a tough slog. Bobby's memory—especially his short-term memory—was still fragile. He often couldn't remember the words for simple objects, and so they had to be repeated to him over and over again. At the hospital he had reached a fourth-grade reading and comprehension level; nonetheless, the doctors told his parents that Bobby's mental age was more like that of a second grader. He could read short sentences, but longer sentences remained a real challenge. He greatly preferred speaking; it was faster and less complicated, and it took less energy, requiring fewer hand and eye movements than reading.

A routine quickly developed. Every morning, John took his son to the hospital for his rehab treatments and exercises. Together they would return home in the early afternoon for a late lunch. Soon thereafter, Lucia returned home to relieve her husband and allow him to go to his office to work. Lucia's primary job, at first, was to review the materials Bobby had learned at the hospital, and then try to reinforce them with repetition drills, plus incorporate something new so that he would be making some progress at home every day. He learned, and he learned quickly. Within two weeks they were using fifth grade materials, and two weeks after that they were using a smattering of middle school materials.

The problem was Bobby's temper, which began to grow even more acerbic and hurtful. One by one his friends stopped visiting.

Because Bobby had gone as far as he could with speech therapy at the hospital, they had to find a new therapist. Lucia found one who was nearby and came highly recommended. Lucia was excited to tell Bobby about him.

"I can meet you and Dad on your way home from the hospital, Bobby," she told him. "We can all have a nice lunch together somewhere and then I can take you to this new therapist. How does that sound?"

Bobby's reaction was not what she had anticipated.

"Why do you treat me like a retard?" he screamed at her. "I know how to talk! I am talking right now."

"But the way you speak is with a flat monotone, slurred, almost incomprehensible," Lucia replied, leaning in close to try to soothe him. "That's why people on the phone often think you're drunk. You are a responsible adult now. You must learn to speak as one."

Bobby pushed his mother away with such force that she lost her balance and fell to the floor, hitting her head against a table as she fell. John had come running when he heard Bobby's screams and witnessed what happened. He strode across the room and slapped Bobby hard across the face.

"What did you do to your mother?" he yelled at his son. "How dare you do that? Don't you know what she's done for you?"

"John, it's all right, honey," Lucia said, slowly rising to her knees.

"No, it's not all right," John fumed. "This sort of behavior has to stop and it has to stop *now!*" John grabbed Bobby and was about to hit him again when Lucia grabbed his legs.

"John, please stop!" she screamed. "Please stop. No violence. It won't do any good."

John let Bobby go with a shove. Bobby lost his balance and keeled over onto the floor. His father glared down at him. "Lucia," he spat, "leave him be. Don't do anything more for him. He doesn't want your help and he sure as hell doesn't appreciate it. Let him remain a cripple and a retard. *That's* what he wants!"

John ran out of the room and out of the house. Bobby dragged himself up onto a sofa and sat there looking scared, drained, and done in. His mother struggled to her feet.

"Are you all right?" she asked her son. She looked for any sign of injuries, but saw nothing. Bobby had gained weight since being home from the hospital—a natural consequence of eating more and exercising less—and that extra weight may have protected him that day. But his lips trembled, he looked pale and sullen, and his eyes were blank, expressionless.

"Do you want to sit in your wheelchair?"

Bobby nodded and struggled to his feet. His mother maneuvered the wheelchair close to him to allow him easier access to it. Bobby sat down and headed for his room. He slammed the door shut, and a few moments later she heard loud music coming from his room.

Alone at last at the end of yet another day, Lucia sank onto the sofa and wept.

She understood the reasons for her husband's acute distress. Peter communicated similar feelings when he came for a visit. Lucia had prepared a memorable dinner for the four of them, but something Peter said set Bobby off and ruined the evening.

The next morning, as Peter was preparing to drive back to Lubbock, he said in confidence to his mother, "Mom, you're spoiling Bobby. He's using his handicap to do what he wants and get what he wants when he wants it. I agree with Dad. Let Bobby live his own life in his own way."

"I can't do that, Peter," Lucia protested. "I can't give up on him any more than I could give up on you or Dad. Don't you remember what Bobby was like? Before the accident? He can be that way again. But to get there, he needs to practice, train, and relearn—harder than ever. Most of all, he needs a family that loves him unconditionally and is there for him whatever happens. It might be easier to give up now and let it be. Is that the kind of life you want for your brother? To forever speak like a child and be in a wheelchair?" She paused a moment to let her questions sink in. "Sure, doing what you suggest would make things easier," she went on, "and more peaceful for the moment, but it would make everything so much harder in the future—for all of us. Do you understand what I'm telling you?"

The look Peter gave indicated that either he did not understand, or he did not accept her line of reasoning. Either way, Peter did not come home again for a long time. Whenever he was invited to come down for a weekend, he begged off with one excuse or another.

The night Bobby threw Lucia to the floor, John returned to the house after being away for several hours. He had gone quiet, was lost deep within himself, and Lucia decided to leave him be. The next morning, however, she broached the subject that was heavy on her mind.

"John," she said, after pouring out two cups of coffee at the kitchen table. "When we got married you said you wanted me to handle the children's education. Can you now let me handle

Bobby's rehab? I don't like what's happening here anymore than you do, but I can't give up on him now no matter what he says or does. I just can't. I will do everything humanly possible to prevent him from living a life as a handicapped person. You understand, don't you?"

John stared down at his cup of coffee as he spoke quietly. "I do understand, honey," he said. "I'm just mad that Bobby can't understand what you've done for him and what you continue to do for him. If you go on like this, you are going to get seriously hurt. Our children are important to both of us, but enough is enough. You mean a lot to me, too, and I can't bear to see you suffer and get hurt. Aren't you sick and tired of fighting all this?"

"No," Lucia said in an equally soft tone. "No, I'm not."

John glanced up. "How can that be? Look at you. You eat next to nothing. You don't sleep at night. You rarely smile. Where do you get the strength and energy to go to work each day, run a chemical company, and then come home and work with a son who usually wants nothing to do with what you are trying to teach him and get him to do?"

"I guess I figure I have no choice," Lucia said.

"Yes, you do," John said. "You just aren't willing to consider the alternatives."

The next day, Lucia went into Bobby's room at the usual hour and informed him that they had some lessons to practice. Predictably, Bobby was none too pleased.

"No," he groused. "I'm not going to do it. You can't make me. I'm going to watch TV and rest."

"Bobby…"

"You can't make me!" he shouted. "Leave me alone!"

"Fine!" Lucia shouted in turn. The iron in her voice caused her son to jerk his head around to face her. "Listen and listen well, Bobby. I'm not doing all this for me. I'm doing it for you. If you don't want me to help you, I won't. You can do whatever you please. But you can't do it here. You'll have to move out and find your own place. I'm not your caretaker. I'm your mother!"

Lucia could see that her words were having the desired effect. Bobby's mouth opened and closed, much like a dying fish at the bottom of a boat. No words came out.

"When your father comes home," Lucia said, "I am going to tell him that you refuse to even try. He'll be furious with you. And he'll agree with every word I am saying to you."

Mother and son glared at each other for several moments. Bobby was the first to blink. "Okay, Mom," he managed at length. "I'll try harder from now on."

He was true to his word. A few evenings later, after a session in the living room, Lucia said goodnight to Bobby and headed for the kitchen. Moments later she heard a heavy thud come from Bobby's room. She found him lying face-down on the floor, struggling to get up. He had been trying to walk on his own and had lost his balance. Lucia's instinct was to run to him and help him up to his feet. But she resisted the impulse. This was something he had to do on his own. She closed the door and went to the bedroom, where she found John in a deep sleep, snoring loudly.

The next morning, at breakfast, Bobby did not mention the previous evening's fall. Lucia wondered how many similar incidents had occurred without her knowing about it.

A few days later, Bobby gave his parents a pleasant surprise. Lucia and John were seated at the breakfast table when Bobby rolled in and stopped his wheelchair farther from the table than he ever had before. As his parents looked on breathlessly, Bobby rose to his feet, and with a smirk on his face, walked the few feet to the table and sat down on his chair.

Lucia shrieked with delight. "Oh my God, Bobby, you did it!"

John broke out in a warm smile and he pumped a fist. Bobby, however, treated what he had done as nothing out of the ordinary. Because he did, Lucia fought off the overwhelming urge to get up and give Bobby a bear hug. She transmitted her admiration and love for her son through her eyes instead.

"John," Lucia gushed, "I say we celebrate tonight. I say we take Bobby out to a nice steak restaurant. He's earned it. We can even invite all our dear friends: Mike and Dee, Ed and Julie, Bob and Shirley, Patti and Todd. What do you say?"

John happily agreed.

That night, at the restaurant, Lucia gave an emotional toast.

"Tonight," she began, "we are toasting Bobby's progress. This morning he walked to the kitchen table. All by himself! We have invited you, all of you, because you are our dearest friends. You've been with us all the way on this journey. You have earned this, too."

She raised her wine glass, tears trickling down her cheeks, ready for this to be a new beginning for Bobby, the start of a new life.

Mike was seated next to Bobby and gave his godson a high-five.

"You'll be out of that wheelchair before you know it," he said, "and causing more mischief than ever. Watch out, Austin!"

Bobby smiled, but contributed little to the festivities. When his steak came, he started devouring it. Lucia told him to slow down and reply to the questions their friends were posing, but Bobby ignored her. He kept right on eating, as though in a feeding frenzy.

"Bobby," Lucia said in mild reproach. "It is more pleasurable to eat your food while having a conversation. Use your knife and fork. Cut off little pieces of meat and chew them slowly. You don't have to rush. Enjoy the evening with us."

Bobby blurted out, loudly, for all to hear, "Leave me alone! I am not retarded, so stop treating me like a child!"

Thankfully, Mike stepped in. "Watch me, Bobby," he said. He cut off a piece of steak and chewed it slowly, as directed by Lucia. "See? It's easy. And it tastes better that way."

Bobby could not ignore Mike. He sat and watched his god-father go at it, but it was clear he was doing so reluctantly. Lucia was deflated. She had hoped Bobby would enjoy the evening more. Perhaps, she thought, she was being too optimistic. Her son's mental age, after all, was that of an elementary school child.

"Bobby is doing fine," Dee and Julie both said to Lucia on the way out to the car. Shirley, who was the quietest, squeezed Lucia's hands, while Patti looked on with empathy. Patti's son Andy had been Bobby's good friend through junior high. Lucia remembered fondly how the boys would have summer math sessions in the Hurs' dining room. But their lives changed immensely over the years and they grew apart. Bobby focused on football, while Andy was more into band and music. Lucia thought about how Andy might have been a good influence on Bobby now, had he not moved to California.

"Bobby looks good and his progress is remarkable," Ed added. He, too, was trying to brighten Lucia's mood and salvage what he could from the evening.

"I see it, too," Bob added.

"That young man is going places," Todd said. "Thanks to you."

There was some truth in their words. Bobby's education was on track. He had finished most of his high school equivalency courses and had started on algebra. His physical progress was also impressive. Five months after returning home he stopped using the wheelchair and started walking on his own. His strength was returning, and he was again projecting the physique of a football player. The problem was his psychological state. That was Bobby's dark side. It remained far behind where it should have been. Most days he seemed unable to control his anger and emotions. The slightest provocation could set him off, no matter who was involved. His friends continued to stay away.

When Bobby cast aside his wheelchair, his doctor instructed him to use a cane instead. This Bobby refused to do. As a result, he took many falls, often landing on his head. Lucia had to speak up.

"I'm not going to take you anywhere," she informed her son, "unless you bring your cane. What are you thinking? You're hurting yourself for no reason."

"I look like an old man when I use the cane," Bobby said. "I don't want to look like an old man."

Lucia put her hands on her hips and glowered at him.

"Bobby, if you fall and hit your head again, you could cause serious damage. You'd be back in bed, maybe forever. You have to use your cane!"

Bobby glowered back. "I don't want to and I don't have to."

"Then you'll have to stay home and not go anywhere."

John was in the living room, listening to the argument unfold.

"Is that what you want?" Lucia pressed.

In reply, Bobby picked up a large clay flowerpot off a table and held it up high. His eyes remained glued to his mother's eyes when he said, "Shit! How long are you going to treat me like a baby? You have no right to tell me what to do!"

With that, he dropped the pot on the floor and it shattered in an ungodly mess.

At the sound of the crash, John stormed into the kitchen over to Bobby and slapped him hard on the face three times.

"How dare you speak to your mother that way!" he shouted. "You wouldn't be here were it not for your mom. She saved you! She brought you back to life! Is this how you repay her? Is this how you show your gratitude? What's *wrong* with you?"

For the first time Bobby took the blows without cowering. He didn't seem so afraid of his father anymore. But tears rolled down his cheeks as he screamed back, "Didn't you hear what this woman said to me? She treats me like a retard! I can't do *anything* I want to do!"

"Shut up!" his father shouted, his eyes wide. "Shut up and apologize to your mother. *Right now!*"

Bobby said nothing.

"If you don't apologize," John snarled, "you will have to leave this house. This is not your house. It's our house, and you are our guest here!"

John's fury was too strong, too bitter, and too concentrated for Bobby to resist any longer. His knees seemed to buckle.

"I'm sorry, Mom," he managed to mumble.

It was a step forward, but Lucia was not about to let her son off the hook so easily. She would no longer tolerate his swearing and his breaking things just because he was angry.

"Pick up your cane and go to your room," she demanded. "You can come out when you are prepared to act like a normal human being."

Bobby complied. As he went limping toward his room, John asked, "Are you okay, honey? You look very pale." He put an arm around her waist and guided her toward a chair.

"Why do you think Bobby is getting more violent and aggressive?" she asked him when she was seated.

"I suppose it's because his heart and mind want to do so much more than his body will allow. He gets frustrated, and he has to take his frustrations out on somebody. You're that person, I'm afraid. The fact that you don't make it easy for him makes him all the more frustrated and angrier."

"That makes sense, of course. Still, I think we should talk to his doctor about it and do more research. The damage to his brain is causing this. I'm convinced of that."

"So am I," John said. "But that does not excuse or justify anything. We can't tolerate his bad behavior. We need to teach him that!"

"Yes," Lucia agreed.

"Can't you stop caring so much?" John said. "For the sake of our peace, can't you let it go when he goes off?"

"No, John, I can't. He's our son and we've got to do whatever it takes to reteach him."

John sighed and sat down beside his wife. "This is all because of me," he said quietly. "None of this would have happened to you if you hadn't come into my life."

Lucia shook her head. Tears welled in her eyes. John held her to him and gently massaged her shoulders as together they braced for the onslaught of more frustration and pain.

# CHAPTER 17

At times it seemed to Lucia as though the war in the Hur household would never end. Mixed in with the hours and days of despair and discouragement were hours and days of great joy and excitement. Bobby would show progress that set her on a cloud. Other experiences set her on edge. Whenever she thought deliverance was finally drawing near, something would infuriate Bobby. One day he would punch her. The next day he would rip off the cover of the book they were studying and throw it at her. Lucia did not tell John about these incidents. There was already enough volatility and tension in the house. But in truth there were days she confessed on the high altar that she wanted to quit, run off somewhere, and do what John had advocated: leave Bobby to his own devices and let him live his own life in his own way. She was sick to death of the vicious cycle of excitement and emotional pain, excitement and physical pain.

She was fast approaching her tipping point. She asked for divine intervention to make her whole again.

During these tumultuous times, Lucia yearned for her mother's advice. How did she raise four children without any major snafus? Yes, Lucia's older brother had been difficult as a child, but he and Lucia's two younger siblings had not caused their parents too much grief. As for Lucia, her parents' only real source of grief was her decision to marry John without their approval, or even their knowledge. In Korean families, such a thing was rarely done and even more rarely appreciated. It was, in effect, a slap in the face of the family, especially since John—an older man with two children—did not appeal to them straightaway. Lucia's mother had cried when she heard of the wedding. Acceptance would take the passage of time and positive experiences. It took many years for them to accept him into the family.

*John.* The mere thought of him and their years together often was enough to console Lucia, and reminiscing about their courtship allowed her an escape into the past whenever necessary.

She remembered one date, not long after they had met. It was early winter in New York City, and John and Lucia had planned to meet outside of Macy's at one in the afternoon. Because the morning had started out relatively warm, Lucia had worn a light coat and open-toed shoes. At the appointed hour, however, John did not show. Thirty minutes passed, then an hour, then another hour. The wind picked up and dark clouds drifted in.

By four o'clock the sun was gone and it was sleeting.

Still Lucia waited. She could have gone inside the store where it was warm. But she worried that if she did, she would miss John, as it was too snowy to see far beyond the windows. In the pre-cellular days, she had no way to call John, she continued to wait outside while her body grew increasingly numb with cold. The prospect of giving up and going home never gained traction. She and John had confirmed the date that morning on the phone; he would show up, she was convinced. She did, however, pray that he was all right driving in such foul conditions. She started worrying that something could have happened. Anxiety churned her stomach.

A little past six o'clock a car drove up and parked. A man got out. It was John.

"Are you still here?" he asked incredulously as he came over and hugged Lucia. "What are you doing here? Why aren't you at home?"

Lucia's teeth were chattering and her whole body had turned icy cold. John took her arm and helped her into the warm car. He took his overcoat and a thick blanket from the back seat and wrapped them around Lucia's shoulders and her frozen feet. "Why aren't you at home?" he asked again when she had warmed up a little.

"We had a date, remember?"

"Of course, I remember," he said. "It's why I'm here. But I did not expect you to be here all this time. Do you know what time it is?"

"What happened?"

"A bad accident on the Triborough. Traffic was backed up for miles and didn't move for hours. There was nothing I could do. On top of that I had a late start from the office due to an emergency. I'm sorry, Lucia."

She took his hand. He could feel her cold flesh, and she could feel the warmth of his. "Don't apologize, John," she said. "As you said, there was nothing you could do. We're together now. That's what's important. Nothing else really matters."

With that, John took her into his arms and kissed her deeply. "You really waited outside in this freezing rain and snow for more than five hours? For me?"

"Of course," she said matter-of-factly. "We had a date, remember?"

Not only did that incident bond Lucia and John as a couple, it pointed the way toward the altar: not long after, they were married. Though different from each other in some respects, including age, they were very much alike in others. Both were strong-willed and independent individuals who complemented each other in ways only they understood. Lucia could not imagine life without John, and John could not imagine a future without Lucia in it.

Thus, with a shaky start, a union was born. Lucia did not tell her parents about her marriage because she knew they would not approve of John. They had in mind someone quite different, someone who was younger and came without the "baggage" of two young children. More importantly, they had envisioned an ambitious young man of means who came highly respected in his chosen profession, preferably medicine or law. They wanted someone who could take care of their little girl, both financially and logistically. Like many parents of their generation, they were less concerned with the emotional underpinnings of the marriage. Love could come later, with time.

Lucia reflected back to events soon after their marriage. John urged the family to move to Austin, where he had acquired a mass of real estate during Austin's building boom. But before long, Austin's real estate market crested, and then took an unpredictable nosedive. John went to Austin to sell and get out before the crash could inflict further damage on the Hurs' finances—but it was too late.

Between John's investments and the market crash, Lucia decided to buy a business to help make ends meet. Once in Austin, the Hurs learned that a small chemical company had come up for sale. The former owner had gotten a divorce and was seeking to sell. Times were becoming tight for the Hur family, but they decided to take a chance. Because John and Lucia were well versed in research and development, they felt confident they could formulate and manufacture superior products for the industrial sanitation industry.

Since they could not afford outside help at first, Peter and Bobby were asked to pitch in. Though still in their preteen years, their personalities were becoming defined. Peter did not want to help out, but, reluctantly, he did. Bobby stubbornly refused. He wanted to go outside and play rather than be stuck inside doing something boring. His mother understood that. And she knew how to handle him.

"Okay, Bobby," she said on one occasion, "if you don't want to help, then don't. But you'll have to come back here again tomorrow."

"Why? What if I finish what I have to do today?"

"Well, if you do that, you won't have to come back. You can do whatever you want to do then."

With that, Bobby was off, working ferociously so that he did not have to return the next day.

Although the economic downturn had left permanent scars on the Hurs' finances, Lucia strongly believed that Bobby and Peter should learn the virtue of hard work and how it can mold and shape them as people.

But raising boys was not easy. There was, for example, the weekend Bobby was invited to a friend's house for a sleepover. He was excited and couldn't wait to go. But Lucia had asked around and discovered that the friend's parents were known to be irresponsible, leaving the children without adult supervision for long stretches of time. Such a scenario was unacceptable to Lucia. She told her son he could not go to the sleepover.

"Why not?" Bobby protested hotly.

"Because I said so," Lucia replied.

"But everyone else is going. Why can't I?"

"I am not comfortable with it, Bobby. I'm sorry. Someday you'll understand."

"No, I won't!" Bobby shouted. "I'll never understand!" He picked up his bag, already packed, and threw it across the room before storming out of the house.

It was the first time Lucia realized that her son had a dark side that went beyond normal youthful angst and edged into rejection and despair.

It would not be the last time.

# CHAPTER 18

Nine months after coming home, Bobby put away his wheelchair for good. He also put away his cane, despite not having fully regained his balance. The consequences were predictable. Once, in a bookstore, he fell over onto a display table, knocking piles of books onto the floor. On another occasion he lost his balance in a restaurant, tipping over a shelf of glasses and breaking them. On yet a third occasion he went with his parents to a buffet. There he tripped and crashed into a stack of plates, shattering them and spilling food on himself and other patrons. His parents begged him to use his cane until he was able to recover his balance, but Bobby steadfastly refused.

"I look like a cripple using a cane," Bobby said. "People stare at me."

Lucia shook her head.

"People are staring at you not because you're using a cane," she said. "People are staring at you because you are creating chaos wherever you go."

Strong words, but they were mild in comparison to the pain Lucia felt from staying up night after night, week after week, month after month, struggling to reteach Bobby the essentials of life. What had happened in the restaurants and in the bookstore happened in the Hur home on nearly a daily basis. Books and pens and pencils were sent flying and papers and cups were thrown around the room, often the result of tantrums and yelling and thrashing. This made it difficult to focus on reading, geography, and math.

In the rare calm moments granted to her, Lucia marveled at what her son was able to learn in spite of the emotional volatility. He was able to master precollege algebra and handle the basic axioms, theorems, and proofs leading to Euclidean geometry. That was where the math learning stopped: advanced math and sciences demanded a level of logic and reasoning that proved too demanding for Bobby's injured brain. Both Lucia and John were relieved when Bobby showed a keen interest in counseling, particularly family counseling. It seemed a better choice than violence and anger, and it brought Bobby a healthy dose of satisfaction.

Somehow, they had survived, and Lucia and John had emerged from the wilds back into civilization. But how could Lucia explain to her son what she had so gladly sacrificed on his behalf, what she had to endure for the love of him? How could she explain that to *anyone*? After all, she could not even convince Bobby to use a cane.

At the buffet, Bobby fell silent for several moments. Then he said, contritely, "I'll be more careful in the future."

"I'm sure you will, but that's not the point," Lucia said. "You haven't fully recovered yet. You're pushing yourself too hard. You're going too fast. Dad and I admire your determination and your courage. But you need to continue your treatments, which means repeating and repeating the drills before you can go the next level. You cannot just bulldoze your way through life."

Bobby nodded in agreement. He knew his mother was right, and although he might be loath to admit it, he was pleased with his progress. Sometime earlier, he had advanced from high school to college equivalents, and his "graduation" had brought great joy. Bobby and his parents still argued, but by now the intensity of the arguments was tempered by the knowledge that meaningful progress was being made.

One day, Lucia asked her son if he would be willing to attend a school outside the home.

"I believe such a learning environment would really help you, Bobby," she said. "You'd still live at home, of course, and either Dad or I would drive you to and from school. But you'd be out on your own. You'd meet new friends. What do you think about that idea?"

Clearly, Bobby liked that idea a lot. His smile was contagious.

In the weeks to follow, Lucia invested considerable time searching for the best option. At length she settled on Austin Community College (ACC), a two-year junior college.

Bobby applied and was accepted.

"One thing, Mom," Bobby said when he received his acceptance papers. "I will go to school by myself. You can drop me off, and you or Dad can pick me up, but that's it. If you start following me around the campus and looking after me, I won't go."

"Agreed. But only if you agree to use your cane. Do we have a deal?"

Bobby nodded slowly. "Deal."

On Bobby's first day of college his mother drove him to school and let him off a reasonable walk from the front entrance. He got out of the car, retrieved his cane and backpack, and headed off. At the front steps he turned around and gave his mother a signal to leave. Lucia waved goodbye and drove off.

But she did not drive far. She parked on a side street, got out, and crept back to the campus, careful not to let Bobby see her. She had to know if Bobby had gone to the right building, if he was interacting properly with his peers, and if he was using his cane to walk. She knew how upset Bobby would be if he caught her spying on him. But she couldn't help herself. She was worried sick.

From what she could tell, however, everything seemed fine. Bobby had gone to the right classroom, and a quick peek through a back door revealed him sitting comfortably with his classmates and preparing to listen to a lecture by a college professor. *His* college professor. Nothing that Lucia saw that morning suggested that her son had been in a coma for three months, gone months unable to drink except through a straw, been barely able to speak for many more months, and then regained speech, but at a child's level. Yet, here was her son sitting at a desk in a classroom in college. *In college!*

Emotion welled up in Lucia as she walked back to the car. If what she had just witnessed was not a miracle, then what is?

Unbeknownst to Bobby, Lucia continued to enjoy this miracle on a near-daily basis, joining Bobby in these classrooms and lecture halls, sitting in the back so he wouldn't notice. In this way, two years of college life passed by.

From that day not too long ago when Lucia learned of her son's accident, she had prayed to God for Bobby's deliverance. Although there had been times when her Catholic faith had been bruised to the bone, it had never been severed. She might have blamed God for abandoning one she loved so dearly, but in the next breath she thanked him for letting Bobby live, for bringing him back to her, for his recovery that was now on a firm footing.

She had made a promise to God that she and Bobby would do good deeds if he recovered, and she intended to keep that promise.

The promise was complicated, though, and Lucia wondered if Bobby knew how much Lucia was giving up to be there for him. She had always wanted a child of her own with John, but had sacrificed that hope for Bobby and Peter. But Bobby didn't seem to recognize Lucia's struggles to provide the best care for him. Or maybe he did, and he wanted to hurt Lucia. She didn't know. "You are not my mother." Those words kept her up at night.

During the early days of Bobby's rehabilitation, Lucia experienced some acute physical discomfort that demanded medical attention. She had been ignoring her physical ailments, including irregular, painful menstrual cycles. She learned she would eventually have to have a complete hysterectomy. Lucia had dreamt that one day she might have a child with John, once the boys were grown and gone. The destruction of this dream was devastating to her. But after considerable prayer and introspection, she took it as a sign from God that she was meant to devote her life to her two sons, especially Bobby, whose fate and fortune had become, for better or worse, inexorably entwined with her own.

On Bobby's first day of school at ACC, Lucia drove to the appointed spot at the appointed hour to pick him up and take him home. When she got there, she saw Bobby in the distance, chatting with some newfound friends. When he saw the car, he waved goodbye to his friends and started limping toward it. That side-to-side limp worried his mother; at times it infuriated her. She realized that the accident had crushed a bone in his leg, making it nearly impossible to walk normally. But if he practiced and if he used his cane at all times—and not just when he knew she was watching him—he might restore his sense of balance and thus minimize the limp. Since he steadfastly refused to do either of those things, it remained a source of conflict between them, and would be for years to come.

"How did it go?" she asked him when he swung himself into the passenger seat. "Did you enjoy the lectures? Did you make new friends?" Although she knew the general answers to these questions, she asked them anyway. Bobby was in a good mood and she wanted to know why.

"Yes," Bobby said in answer to all three questions. "It went well. It went very, very well."

"How so?"

"There are girls here."

Lucia caught her breath. She was not surprised Bobby had mentioned girls. All young men talk about girls, and Bobby was, after all, a handsome man with physical appeal. His emotional state, however, was more like that of a middle school student than a college student. That was why the subject of girls had caught her a bit off guard.

"Yes, there are," she acknowledged. "There are many of them here on campus. Anyone you like?"

"Maybe one or two," he said.

"What about the lecture in your first class? Did you understand it?"

"Sure. It was easy. You've already taught me that stuff."

"Good. I'm glad to hear it," she said. "So, do you think you can handle this?"

"Of course, I can!" Bobby exclaimed, his voice brimming over with confidence and excitement.

"Excellent. Then here is what I suggest: lose some weight and learn to speak more clearly, without slurring your words or speaking in a monotone. Girls like guys who are not only handsome and fit, but who are eloquent. You already have the tools you need at your disposal. You just refuse to use them."

"I am eloquent," he declared. "I can write good poems. Girls like poetry."

It was true that Bobby had a keen interest in reading and writing poetry. He was quite good at it, as his English teachers in high school had confirmed. During his recovery, Lucia had encouraged Bobby to again try his hand at writing poetry. She thought she might be able to interpret his innermost thoughts and emotions through his writing. Her initial attempts, however, invariably ended in frustration. At first, the beginning of each poem seemed out of sync with the ending, causing confusion to the point of distraction and incomprehension. But as time went on, and as his mental state improved, so did his literary prowess. Lucia began collecting his poems, and when she had enough, she had them printed in book form and distributed to family, friends, teachers, and anyone else she felt might be inspired by Bobby's words. She did this to give Bobby a sense of accomplishment and to motivate him to ever greater heights. She also did this to encourage other mentally and/or physically challenged people to express their individuality in their own way and to no longer see their disability as a handicap.

Whether it was the poetry or whether it was his parents repeatedly telling him that he was not handicapped but instead in recovery, Bobby's confidence in himself and his future grew to the point that Lucia started contemplating the plausibility of her son attending a four-year college. She felt sure he could do it, and she wanted him to experience the benefits of life on a university campus—the life he had once been heading for.

She went to see Bobby's advisor at ACC.

"Don't you think he's doing well?" she asked him.

"Yes, I do," said the middle-aged, slightly balding professor of English. He glanced down at a wealth of papers on his desk. "His grades are better than average. Frankly, he's doing better than many of us here at ACC expected."

"Is he doing well enough to go to a four-year university?"

The advisor glanced up. "You're serious, aren't you?"

"Of course, I am serious," Lucia said. "Why wouldn't I be?"

The professor let a moment pass. Then he said, "Are you not satisfied with the way things are? I just told you that no one here thought he could do as well as he has. Of course, he's had immense help from his teachers, which likely would not be the case at a university. Isn't what you have here enough?"

"Frankly, no." Lucia said. "It's not enough. Not for my son. Since by your own admission he's doing well here at ACC, what's to stop him from going on to a university?"

"Well, for one thing, he's not exactly treated like the other students. He has certain advantages here that he might not have at a university."

Lucia knew what he was referring to. When Bobby had been accepted at ACC, he was granted certain accommodations as a result of his reduced cognitive abilities. Community colleges have policies regarding "special needs" students, and Lucia convinced ACC that her son was indeed handicapped and needed such accommodations.

Lucia did not appreciate the professor's tone, nor what she took as the insinuation that Bobby was receiving better grades than he deserved as a result of his handicapped status. The tone suggested that other professors had taken pity on Bobby and had graded him accordingly.

As soon as she was able, Lucia extricated herself from that meeting and went to see Dr. Morledge. After complaining to him about ACC's unwillingness to help her son beyond what was obligatory, she said, "Don't you think our society should be more proactive in helping children get a college education? Don't we have a moral obligation to do that? Can't I expect for my son to be able to attend a four-year university?"

The doctor pondered those questions before folding his hands on his desk and leaned toward Lucia.

"Lucia, may I be frank with you?"

"Of course, Doctor."

"If you and John truly want Bobby to attend a university, you must first make him independent of you. That means not jumping in and helping with every little thing he comes up against. He must learn to think and act on his own. Your intentions are good—no one can deny that—but you may not be helping him in the long run. If Bobby can learn to live without that help, then maybe he can make it work in college."

Lucia had to admit to herself that what the doctor was saying made sense. John had more or less said the same thing to her, and it was something she intuitively realized was true. But her heart did not always listen to what her mind told her.

That evening, she told John what the doctor had said. Not surprisingly, he immediately agreed with Dr. Morledge. The thought of Bobby being on his own far away seemed not to unsettle him. Lucia decided to put the question directly to her son.

"Bobby," she asked him that same evening, "do you want to go to college in Lubbock? You can, you know. But if you do, you will have to do everything all by yourself. There will be no one to help you. That includes Peter."

As his parents had anticipated, the prospect of living apart from them and on his own appealed mightily to their son. From that moment on, there was no question that Bobby would go to a university. And there was no question where he would go. Texas Tech offered the best option. Although Peter could not check in on Bobby every day, at least he was there. And Lubbock was a city Bobby knew and liked, and Texas Tech was a school he was familiar with. A number of his high school friends lived near or on campus. In addition, Lucia had made initial inquiries and discovered that the university would make special accommodations for Bobby.

As a preliminary major, Bobby selected family counseling. It was a subject Bobby understood, and it was one he liked. Science or engineering—subjects for which the university was more renowned—would be, Lucia feared, too challenging.

So, Bobby became a college student. He had been one at ACC, of course, but now he was enrolled in a "mainstream" university that commanded respect in Texas and across the country. His parents were very proud of him. He had gone from lying in a vegetative state following a horrific automobile accident to sitting in a Texas Tech classroom as a true Red Raider.

Bobby had come so far. But as Lucia and John, not to mention Bobby's doctors, knew in those deep, dark places, he still had a long way to go.

# CHAPTER 19

The evening of the day Bobby left with Peter to move to Lubbock, Lucia and John went out to celebrate Bobby's independence—and their own. It had been a long, long time since the two of them had gone to a nice restaurant for a quiet and restful meal together.

They had just sat down at their table when John announced he was feeling dizzy. Before he finished speaking, he fell unconscious to the floor.

The restaurant was thrown into pandemonium. Someone called 911 and within minutes an ambulance arrived. The paramedics took him straight to a hospital, where he was admitted to the emergency room. A number of tests were run, all of which were inconclusive. The doctors found nothing amiss beyond factors that were stress-related. He was discharged soon thereafter and sent home with strict orders to rest.

Lucia was relieved beyond measure to learn that nothing serious seemed to have befallen her husband. Her concerns returned, however, when John's condition did not improve after a couple of days of rest. He still felt dizzy, and he could not tolerate bright light. He kept the curtains and blinds of the house closed tight, and could barely walk, or even stand. Lucia found the timing of this to be cruel to the extreme. She did not know what to do, or even what to think.

Nor did John.

Normally an industrious and energetic man, he was used to waking up early and heading to the kitchen to put on the coffee and make breakfast. Now, he could do little beyond lying in bed in a dark room. He felt not only dizzy but nauseous; he could barely eat. Getting up and going to the bathroom became a marathon challenge.

The doctors weren't much help. Since they offered no diagnosis, John had no prognosis, no medicine or treatment methodology to help make him better. Lucia therefore took matters into her own hands. As she had done when Bobby lay comatose in the hospital, she gathered whatever information about John's condition she could from periodicals, books, medical journals, and, this time, the internet. She did all of this research at home after work, deep into the night—night after night—for weeks. The hours were so long and demanding, John became concerned about her health.

"Do you feel as though you're going to get sick?" he asked her one day.

"No. Why do you ask?"

"Because you don't look well. Your eyes are all bloodshot. You act as though you're on your last legs."

"Sorry, honey. It can't be helped."

"Yes, it can," John insisted. "One of us has to stay well. We can't both be bedridden. We have too much to do, too much to complete. You need to get your rest."

"I'll rest once I understand your symptoms and find the cure."

One day, after yet another round of extensive research, Lucia concluded that a combination of three medications—Dilantin,

Thorazine, and Meclizine—would address her husband's symptoms. She called her father, the famous heart surgeon, to discuss her findings. After studying that class of medications and their interactions with one another, he concluded it was worth a try and wrote out the prescriptions.

Three days after starting the meds, John's condition began to improve. Lucia was relieved, but still she needed to understand the reasons for John's illness if she were to prevent it from reoccurring.

She made an appointment with a renowned vertigo specialist at the Mayo Clinic and discussed the matter with him. He agreed that John's condition could have been induced by stress. He was surprised to learn that Lucia had given John the three medications and asked her to keep him informed about John's progress. He added that in the future, he would prescribe the same medications for patients exhibiting similar symptoms. Because at the time there was no medical name for what John had, the doctor gave it the name *migrainous vertigo*. The name stuck. He did not offer any instructions other than to use the medications any time John's symptoms returned.

John continued to take the meds. Three days later he was able to go to the bathroom by himself. Two days after that he could walk into the living room and open the curtains. He reported that his headaches were gone, and his dizziness had abated. Two days later, he was eating fruit and drinking juice, a sure indication that his nausea was gone. Two months after he had been admitted to the hospital emergency room, he was back to his old self and daily routine.

To Lucia, it was a relief that John had taken ill after Bobby left for Texas Tech University. Having to take care of them both would have been extremely difficult.

"This happened because you haven't been taking care of your-self," she told her husband. "You've been drinking too much coffee and under too much stress. This has to stop. You have to cut down on stress and your work hours. You're vulnerable now, and because you are, you could catch anything."

"And so can you," John countered. "You're the one under stress. You're the one working too hard. You never rest. Ever. And it kills me to see you that way. Don't worry about me. Worry about yourself."

And so, it went. Both John and Lucia realized their words would not have a lasting impact: they both would continue to work too hard and take too little rest. Such was the basis of their love for each other—words could express a portion of that love, but the greater part was expressed by their devotion to each other, to their family, and to their livelihoods. On any given evening they would sit at the dinner table or at a restaurant and talk for hours about their strategies, hopes, and expectations. Rarely was there a moment when they were not sharing a thought or idea with each other. A number of their friends had commented that Lucia and John acted like a young couple, still very much in love. Comments like that made them smile.

After Bobby left home and John's medical condition improved, Lucia threw herself into her work. Whether from her hard labor or because it was the right time in the business cycle, both revenues and profits began increasing handsomely. Lucia had by this time gained a reputation for honesty and good business practices that her clients admired. It was known throughout the industry that she would not cut deals; she would treat all customers the same, and she would go the extra mile for any one of them. Her company's products also gained a reputation for unsurpassed quality and consistency, supported by outstanding customer service that was unmatched in the industry. If a customer tried to strong-arm her or play games with accounts payable, he was told to shop elsewhere. Lucia approached every aspect of her work as if her life depended on it, which, in many ways, it did.

The days were long and demanding, to the point that male clients and staff marveled at how a female CEO could accomplish so much in a day's work. Part of Lucia's drive could be traced to her father's advice to always strive for success. Another part stemmed from her love for her family—Peter and Bobby, of course, but also John. He was the mainstay, her safe harbor in a stormy sea of change and challenge. During the business day the mere thought of him either calmed her or steeled her resolve to tackle whatever obstacle confronted her. When she finished work in the late evening and drove home, he would be there, waiting, a glass of wine already poured, a candle lit on the table, and a delicious dinner in the oven.

That was the happiest time of the day for Lucia. She could unwind, sip a glass of wine, and unload the events of the day onto someone who truly cared. So, too, would she listen with rapt attention as John debriefed her on the events of his day. Often, she would sit back and sigh deeply, joyful in the knowledge that her life was blessed as long as John was in it.

She was at peace, at least for the moment.

Texas Tech followed the nationwide standard regarding handicapped students, but no more than that. The school's policies made no special mention of TBI or other brain injuries. Ostensibly, the administration assumed that when a student was admitted, he could take care of himself. And if he was unable to do that, then perhaps Texas Tech was not the right college for him.

At first, it seemed, Texas Tech was not the right college for Bobby. From almost the day he arrived on campus, Bobby developed a reputation for being a troublemaker. He harassed his professors, he was rude to his fellow students, and his generally sullen demeanor caused nearly everyone to give him a wide berth. As his isolation heightened, his sense of loneliness and detachment intensified—and the problems increased.

Several months into the fall semester Lucia received a call from the dean.

"Mrs. Hur," he said, "I must ask you to come up here and take Bobby home. He is causing too much trouble. All of his professors are complaining that he is disrupting their classes. This simply cannot continue. You must take him home."

Lucia was momentarily speechless.

"Professors are complaining about Bobby?" she asked at length. "I find that hard to believe. Bobby would never be mean to a professor."

"That's not it. Bobby isn't being mean to them."

"What, then?"

The dean went on to explain that Bobby had become infatuated with certain female professors and was following them around campus. When they asked him to stop, he turned a deaf ear. For one professor the issue had reached a point where she refused to teach her class until Bobby was gone. Other professors had expressed similar concerns and demands, the dean said.

Lucia was not unduly surprised. Nurses at the hospital had made the same sort of complaints against Bobby when he was a patient there, but none of them had pressed any kind of charge against him. The nurses were used to such behavior from patients with severe brain damage. And Lucia knew from her own research that traumatic brain injury causes people to exhibit behavior that otherwise would have been unthinkable to them. Often the bad behavior is of a sexual nature, as it was in Bobby's case. Groping, pinching, and sexual innuendo were assaults to a woman's dignity that Bobby would never have contemplated before his TBI.

"Why are these professors complaining to you?" Lucia asked the dean. She could think of nothing else to say. "Isn't it normal for a young man to be infatuated with an attractive, intelligent female professor? It seems innocent enough to me."

"Your son's gestures and words could hardly be classified as innocent, Mrs. Hur," he said. "They don't just involve flowers and love poems."

"Has Bobby done something bad?"

"Depends on what you mean by bad. What he is doing is harassment, plain and simple, and that's bad enough. But we fear he will someday soon decide to take everything one step further. You know what I mean by that. And if he does, are you prepared to accept the full consequences of his actions? It will be your liability. He has been warned, and with this telephone call, so have you."

"I understand. Let me talk to Bobby and I'll get back to you," Lucia said.

"Please call him right away, Mrs. Hur," the dean insisted.

Lucia took a few minutes to compose herself before placing a call to her son. Without allowing any opportunity for Bobby to interject a word, she reviewed with him the accusations the dean had put forth.

"Listen, Bobby, and listen carefully," she concluded in no uncertain terms. "This kind of behavior is inappropriate and unacceptable, and will not be tolerated either by the university or by me. If you continue to harass your female professors, you will be kicked out of college and sent home. I know how much you don't want that. I know how much you don't want to live with your father and me again and have us tell you what to do every hour of every day. But I promise you it *will* happen if you don't grow up and start acting your age."

Immediately upon saying that, Lucia regretted her words. Bobby had not acted his age since the accident. She wasn't sure he was capable of acting his age, or would be ever again. But she had no choice. Given what was at stake, she had to play every card she held.

"Do you understand what I am telling you?" she pressed.

"I do, Mom," Bobby said at length. His voice was low, tense. "I'm sorry. It won't happen again."

"It best not."

Four days later Lucia received another call from the dean.

"It's happened again, Mrs. Hur," he said with a heavy sigh.

"What's happened again? Be specific."

"Bobby and one of his professors got into an argument. It started out innocently enough but soon got ugly. Bobby ended up calling her a terrible name and threatened to kill her."

"Bobby threatened to *kill* her?"

"In a sense," the dean said. "What he said to her was, 'You're lucky you're a professor; otherwise you'd be killed.'"

"Yes, but..."

"No buts, Mrs. Hur. Bobby is hereby expelled from this university. I'm sorry." And he hung up.

Lucia sat down at her desk and buried her face in her hands. Every instinct told her what had really happened: Bobby had become involved in a discussion with a professor who didn't like him. Things got out of hand when the professor called him something unpleasant, such as retard. Even the mere hint of an insensitive remark was all it took to push her son to say something he didn't truly mean. Lucia knew better than anyone that Bobby had serious issues that could lead to violence. But only toward her. She could not fathom him threatening bodily harm to anyone else and meaning it.

But for the moment, that was neither here nor there. The university seemed determined to get rid of a student it regarded as a troublemaker and had come up with an excuse to oust him. Lucia could either accept the decision or fight it.

She decided to fight it. Early the next morning she was on the road from Austin to Lubbock. The next afternoon she met with the dean and two other senior administrative officials. Also present, was the professor whom Bobby had allegedly threatened. The four of them sat together on the opposite side of a long rectangular table from Lucia.

Once they were all seated, Lucia launched in.

"I know my son has serious issues," she admitted straightaway. "You know why he does. You know what he has been through, what he has survived. Not many people could have achieved what he has achieved. Nonetheless, his cognitive abilities are not yet what they should be. He does things and says things that may not be appropriate. But he's not a dangerous person. You don't seriously believe that he would purposely do harm to one of your staff, do you?"

The ensuing silence suggested that the two men and two women facing her did indeed believe that.

Lucia met their gaze. "What grounds do you have for expelling my son?" she asked.

The dean slowly shook his head.

"We've been through all that, Mrs. Hur," he said wearily.

"I'm sorry, but you haven't. Not to my satisfaction," she said. "And I doubt to the satisfaction of the courts. If you can't come up with a plausible reason for expulsion, my husband and I will have no choice but to seek redress through the legal system."

Those words struck a chord. The four administrators stole a glance at each other and shifted uneasily in their seats. Perhaps, thought Lucia, they were seeing in their mind's eye what she wanted them to see: a damning newspaper article decrying the unfair expulsion of a handicapped student. Such negative publicity was anathema to a public organization.

Sensing she had them where she wanted them, Lucia changed tack.

"You can't kick out a student who has accomplished what Bobby has," she reiterated, her voice low, confidential. "You have an obligation to him and to our society to do everything you can to educate him, not just with what they read in books and hear in class. As an institution, you are obliged to provide education to *all* students. Isn't that true?"

Lucia's line of reasoning had no noticeable impact. She looked hard at the professor who claimed to have been threatened by Bobby. Her gaze made him fidget and squirm in his chair.

"Tell me this, professor," Lucia said in a steely tone. "Would you kick him out of this university if he was your son and was in the same situation?"

The professor had looked away. The ice in Lucia's tone brought him back.

"Well, would you?" Lucia demanded to know.

When the professor offered no reply, Lucia said in a modified tone, "I thought I had lost my son. I thought he would never come back after the accident. Can't you understand that?" Her question was directed at the professor, but addressed to them all. "Can't you see all this from Bobby's perspective? Consider, just for a moment, what all has happened to him. Do you seriously think, after everything he has gone through to get to this point, that his parents could just sit back and watch their son be expelled from this institution? Yes, I admit, he can be cantankerous at times, and a bit of a nuisance. That's because of the damage done to his brain as the result of the accident. But he's no threat to anyone. Despite all that he's been forced to endure, he is getting adequate grades. You said that yourselves. And he hasn't physically harmed anyone, has he? Can't you find it in your hearts to give him another chance? Can you really be that cold-blooded and cruel?"

Silence pervaded the room after Lucia finished speaking. Following a meaningful span of reflection, the dean requested that Lucia leave the room to allow the four officials to discuss the matter amongst themselves in private.

In the waiting area, Lucia sipped a glass of water a secretary brought her. That water was the only sustenance she had taken in that day, which was one reason her arms and legs were trembling. The other reason was the acute stress she felt in every fiber of her being. She was scared not for herself, but for Bobby.

After a twenty-minute wait she was summoned back into the dean's office.

"Mrs. Hur," the dean said in a tone that was at once both somber and conciliatory, "my colleagues and I are touched by what you have said. Very touched indeed. You spoke eloquently and cogently on behalf of your son, a young man of promise whom we now better understand deserves extra considerations. We are therefore prepared to offer you what we believe is an eminently reasonable compromise. If you will assure us that your son will never again be involved in these kinds of incidents on this campus, we will agree to withdraw our notice of expulsion and give him another chance. But there is a condition attached to our offer."

"What is the condition?" Lucia asked.

"In return, you must promise us that if another incident should occur at any time in the future, you will take your son home. No questions. No arguments. No protests. No nothing. Are you prepared to accept such terms?"

Lucia blinked. "What assurances do I have that someone in this university won't contrive an incident to get Bobby expelled?"

"You have my word that won't happen," the dean said. "That is the only assurance I can give you and the only assurance you should need."

"Then my answer is yes," Lucia responded without hesitation. "If I have your promise, then you have mine."

"Very well. Consider it done."

After she left the dean's office, Lucia went to meet Bobby in front of his dorm, as they had arranged. He looked sad and withdrawn, and she felt sorry for him.

"It seems," she said as she walked up to him, "that my mission in life is making everything harder for you. Do you want to go home with me?"

Bobby shook his head. "No, Mom. I want to stay here. I'm happy here. Have I been kicked out?"

"I take it, then, that you don't want to be expelled?"

"No, Mom. I just finished telling you. I want to stay here. I want my college degree. I've worked hard for it. Now, *please* answer my question. Have I been kicked out?"

"First, I must ask *you*: do you understand why the school felt justified in wanting to kick you out?"

Bobby shoved his hands in his pants pockets and looked down at his shoes. "They claim I acted badly."

"Did you? Act badly?"

"Maybe. But the professor started it. He called me an idiot."

Lucia let out a sustained sigh.

"That was wrong of him," she said. "Very wrong. But that does not excuse what you did. You can't lash out and curse people every time something goes against you. You certainly can't do that in a classroom setting. And you can't follow female professors around campus and give them flowers and write love poems to them. Do you understand the consequences of such foolish behavior?"

"I do, Mom," Bobby said softly. "I do understand that. I just want another chance to prove myself. To you and to the university. Just give me one more chance. It's all I ask."

"Well, you have it. The university has agreed to give you that chance."

Bobby's jaw dropped. "Thank God!" he said.

"But you know the conditions, Bobby. There can be no more inappropriate behavior, no more complaints. If there is just one, I have given my word that I will come up here and take you home. For good, this time. Do you understand?"

"I do understand, Mom," Bobby said, his voice shaking slightly. "Thank you. I won't let you down, I promise."

And he didn't. Despite an occasional hiccup, Bobby managed to graduate from Texas Tech University with a bachelor of arts degree in family counseling. After the graduation ceremonies, his parents threw a bash in honor of their son's accomplishments. Many people came, including members of the admissions committee. Messages of congratulation poured in from around the state and beyond, including those from hospital staff in both Austin and Lubbock.

The Hur family indeed had much to celebrate. No one with traumatic brain injury who had lain in a comatose state for three months and who had been dismissed by medical professionals as a vegetable had ever graduated from Texas Tech University.

# CHAPTER 20

lthough Bobby was making progress on a scale few people could have anticipated, Lucia understood that he still had a long way to go. No doubt, many obstacles remained. He was not yet thirty years of age. Statistically, he still had two-thirds of his life ahead of him, and it was up to her—not John, not Peter, not any of his friends— to help her son navigate the rest of it.

At the time, John and Lucia were involved in several civic organizations in Austin designed to help Asians assimilate into Texas society. It was no easy matter for an outsider to move to Texas and assimilate with Texans. Texans tend to be politically conservative and suspicious of outsiders.

Come Join us with Elvis!

Hur's 6ᵗʰ Annual Special
"Needy Gift Project"
Dance-Singing Party with Elvis

Date: Dec 8ᵗʰ Saturday 2013
Time: 6:00 PM
Location: Hur's Ranch Residence
6620 West Creekview Drive, Austin, TX 78736

*Many Raffle Drawings!*

Dress Attire: Holiday Cocktails &
Potluck Welcome!

RSVP: Lucia.hur@hurchem.com or (512) 731-3922
Admission: 2 x Xmas Gift for the Needy child ~

Gender/Age /Content tag on the gift.
Example: Label tag ~ Female or Unisex (5-13 yrs. old) Board Game
Maximum $25- $30 per gift for kids; $ 30 - $40 per teenagers

Hence, in 1998 John and a couple of other accomplished Asians, David Chan and Tommy Hodinh, formed a nonprofit business organization titled the Texas Asian Chamber of Commerce

(TACC). Lucia volunteered to serve on the founding board, a position she held from 1998 to 2012.

**TEXAS ASIAN CHAMBER OF COMMERCE**
## Press Release

Contact: Lucia C. Hur
Phone: 512-420-8777 FOR IMMEDIATE RELEASE
5:30 p.m., December 28, 2004

### TSUNAMI MOBILIZES ASIAN AMERICANS

**Texas Asian Foundation, sister organization of the Texas Asian Chamber of Commerce takes initiative to aid victims of disaster in South Asia.**

**Austin, Texas, December 28, 2004.** The shock of unimaginable human toll, as well as destruction of even rudimentary living amenities, has impelled so many to rise up to the occasion. The Asian American community in Texas led by the Texas Asian Chamber of Commerce and its sister organization, Texas Asian Foundation, have launched a community wide effort to help the victims of the consequences of the infamous Tsunami that has visited upon South Asia.

The public, Asian and non-Asian communities, is invited to participate in the fund raising campaign. Contributions are requested to be sent to the Texas Asian Foundation c/o Prosperity Bank, 8770 Research Blvd., Austin, TX 78758, marked "Memo Tsunami Fund", or to mail to Texas Asian Chamber of Commerce, 8222 Jamestown Dr., Suite A113, Austin, TX 78758.

Queries may be directed to 512-420-8777 or cell 751-3922.

-End-

Many Texans would be on edge around a Korean-American woman who was chief executive officer of an international chemical manufacturing company and served on the board of civic-minded organizations such as the TACC. But with John's support Lucia forged ahead, and in so doing, made a name for herself.

John and Lucia wanted to make a difference. They wanted to help other Asian businesses facing similar challenges from Texas prejudice. They also wanted to make a difference in their own family. Lucia believed that devoting herself to public service was payback for all the good tidings and blessings she had received from God. It was also the fulfillment of the promise she had made, that she would help others if God would take care of Bobby and the family.

On one occasion, in her capacity as a TACC chairperson, Lucia hosted a major fundraising event in Austin to which the city's celebrities were all invited. It was to be a gala affair, and Lucia wanted Bobby to have an important role in it. She wanted him to feel pride in himself and in his environs; she also wanted him to rub elbows with influential people. She therefore asked him to use his creative abilities to compose a prayer that he would then read at the opening ceremony.

Bobby agreed and went right to work on his assignment. Lucia found, however, that the prayer he ultimately composed was out of step with the spirit of the event. She asked him to redo the prayer, using the guidelines she had originally provided him.

"Don't treat me like a child," Bobby protested. "I did exactly what you asked me to do." He held up a sheet of paper. "This is the prayer I composed and this is the prayer I intend to read. If you don't like it, I'm sorry. But it is what it is."

His mother's jaw dropped.

"Why on earth do you say things like that?" she asked him. "All I'm asking is that you redo the prayer so it fits in better with the theme of the event. Is that really too much to ask?"

"Yes, it is," Bobby insisted. "I am sick to death of your constant nagging and interference in my life. You're always insisting on your way of doing things. You dictate what I should do and then you correct everything I do. You're a control freak!"

Lucia felt her blood rise. She had to struggle to keep her voice calm and measured.

"Oh really? Is that a fact? Than tell me this, Bobby: Who else is here for you? Who else has your back, no matter what you do or who you insult? Who else is there to fight for you? Who else wants to see you succeed the way I do? Can you name one person other than Dad?"

Bobby went silent.

"I thought so," Lucia muttered.

"If I do the prayer the way you want me to," Bobby said, "then it is your prayer, not mine. I don't want to do your prayer."

"Bobby," Lucia sighed, "a chance to do something important and memorable like this doesn't come around very often. This is not about me. Not at all. This is entirely about you. It would mean a lot to you and to many other people if you were to compose and read the right kind of prayer. Would you like me to ask someone else to do it?"

Bobby slowly shook his head. "No. You win, Mom. I'll do it your way."

Not only did Bobby do it, he did it well. He revised his prayer to suit the occasion, and for his good effort he received high marks from virtually everyone in attendance. In the midst of the accolades, his parents saw an element in their son that they had not seen since the accident. It was a glint of pride. Pride in his words and pride in himself for delivering them on cue and on target.

It was a day none of them would soon forget.

Several weeks later Bobby asked his mother what she would like for her birthday. This was something he did for her birthday, Mother's Day, and Christmas. The question brought out a sweet side of their son that they had seen regularly prior to the accident, but only rarely since then.

"Do you want to give me something I really want?" Lucia asked.

"Yes, of course I do," Bobby said. "Name it."

"Let me clean your house. That is what I truly want."

When Bobby graduated from Texas Tech, his parents had rented for him a modest condominium twenty minutes from their own house. At first, Lucia had wanted him to live at home to make the ongoing rehab easier to accommodate. But Bobby pleaded his case by arguing that he was no longer a child but an adult who deserved to live on his own.

"If you do that," Lucia warned, "all of the conveniences you take for granted will be gone. Are you prepared to accept that?"

"I am," Bobby said. "I need to act like an adult because I am one. If I make mistakes, I'll learn from those mistakes. I can't make mistakes if you and Dad are doing everything for me."

This was a difficult argument for his parents to challenge. Several weeks later they helped move their son into the condo.

But when they began to move furniture around and dig into his possessions, Bobby became angry. He was adamant that these items were his and that he would be responsible for the upkeep and the interior design of his own home. Still today, in fact, the issue of the condo's upkeep and maintenance has proven to be a sore point.

Lucia knew that she would be unable to clean anything in it without his permission. So as a birthday gift, she asked for that permission. Bobby agreed, and that made Lucia happy. The work she invested in making his living quarters neat and tidy was, for her, a true labor of love.

Since Bobby at this stage did not yet have a job, his parents supported him financially. There was a problem, however. In Texas it is difficult to get around without a car. Most public transportation systems are mediocre at best, so without a car, a Texan is beholden to the kindness of close friends and family members. Although there was a special transit system called Metro providing door-to-door service that Bobby could have used as a handicapped person, he refused to use it. To do so, he believed, would brand him as "a cripple," and that was not to his liking.

"I passed the driving test at the hospital," he reasoned. "So why won't you get me a car? Do you think I can't drive one?"

At the hospital Bobby was made to believe that he had passed the balance test and the driving simulation test, and he used these accomplishments as leverage to get a car. St. David's has one of the best and most rigorous programs in the state for rehabilitating potential drivers. War veterans mangled in combat make use of this center to once again obtain a license, and individuals suffering from psychological disorders also participate in this program. Once the officials assess a patient's physical and psychological profile, they offer a driving simulation test. If the patient passes the test, he or she is awarded a driving certificate. Bobby had managed to pass this test.

Lucia, however, did not see eye to eye with either Bobby or the hospital. She remained unconvinced that her son possessed the necessary skills and cognitive ability to operate a motor vehicle. He had, after all, almost gotten himself killed in a car accident. Despite great leaps forward, his judgment remained unstable. His reflexes were still questionable, much slower than the average person's. If he found himself in an emergency situation, she seriously doubted he would react the way other adults would react. She therefore denied him the car, not once but multiple times. John agreed. The issue would become a constant source of antagonism between parents and son in the years to follow.

Soon thereafter, Peter came home with a lovely young blonde woman and announced that he wanted to marry her. She was a Canadian nurse who worked in the same Lubbock hospital as Peter and Neil.

"What do you like about her?" Lucia asked.

"What's not to like?" Peter responded wryly. "She's pretty and easygoing, and she makes me happy." Of greater importance, Peter confided to Lucia that Stephanie was very much like Lucia in doing what he called "little sweet things" that he considered endearing, such as putting love notes inside the box lunches that she made for him. "We have a lot of fun together," Peter concluded. "We make a great couple, don't you think?"

"You do," his father agreed. During the several days Peter was home, John had warmed up to his future daughter-in-law. He admired her intellect and the respect she held for her elders. He had never before had a daughter; now he would, of a sort.

John and Lucia gave their blessing to the marriage, a decision they would never come to regret. Peter was happy.

Having the two boys gone from home and being on their own was like a honeymoon period for Lucia and John. John was retired and took great delight in preparing a dinner for his wife when she returned home from work. Most evenings the dinner was accentuated by a glass or two of wine, flickering candlelight, and a dish of cheese and crackers.

Her husband's sweet attentions pleased Lucia no end, but what truly touched her heart were some words spoken to her in confidence by a close friend of hers named Mike Shultz. Mike had been instrumental in helping John maintain his sanity at the rehab hospital. Mike, in effect, had provided a shoulder for John to lean on. On a regular basis he showed up at the physical therapy room to watch John and Bobby work out and to offer encouragement. One day, John and Mike decided to go to a café for a cup of coffee. There John poured out his soul to Mike.

"What John told me," Mike said to Lucia the next day, "was that after the accident he had complained to God over and over again. He was just getting over the horror of what had happened to Susan, and now the same sort of horror was happening all over again. He could have lost Bobby, and he swears he would have lost him if it hadn't been for you. He also said he could not have survived were it not for you. He doesn't have your stamina and he doesn't have your persistence. He was just too mentally exhausted and drained to go through it a second time. He said he would have just given up."

Lucia swallowed hard. "John has never told me this," she confessed quietly. "Did he say anything else?"

Mike nodded. "He did. And he was close to tears when he said it." Lucia took a deep breath to squash the rising emotions. "John told me that you had never gone through anything this rough in your life, and it was all because of him that you have had to suffer. When he first met you, you looked so weak, thin, and needy; all he wanted to do was wrap you in his arms and take care of you. Now you're the one taking care of him. And Bobby. And Peter. And almost everyone who has become close to you. And you're doing all this while running a successful business. He doesn't know how you manage to do it all and do it all so well without ever complaining. He doesn't know where you draw your strength and resolve from. Most of all, he doesn't know how you are so capable of loving so much. What he does know is that he loves you with all his heart and soul, and always will."

Lucia avoided Mike's eyes as her friend fell silent. Her own eyes filled with unshed tears. She had never heard such words from John. She had never felt the depth of his emotion and his devotion to her and their family. She knew it was there, but he had never expressed it. Now she understood, fully.

"Thank you for telling me this, Mike. It means a lot to me. More than I can properly express."

"You're welcome, Lucia," Mike replied. "I hope John doesn't feel I've betrayed his trust by telling you all this. I felt it was something you needed to hear."

Lucia reached out and squeezed Mike's hand.

"John doesn't need to know that you told me anything," she said. She then got up to embrace her friend. "But I can assure you I will never forget what you said today. As you know, John is a man of few words. More often than not, he keeps words and emotions bottled up inside him."

Later that afternoon when she arrived home, she went up to her husband and kissed him full on the lips.

"I want you to call Kerry and B.J.," she said, referring to two friends who had been bugging John to join them on the golf course.

"Why?" John asked. "What's the occasion?"

"No occasion. I just happen to know that they've been after you to play golf with them."

"So?"

"So tomorrow you are playing golf with them all day. No arguments, please. Tomorrow evening I am cooking dinner for you."

John gave her a look of surprise. "Why? What's going on?"

"Love is going on," she answered with a smile.

# CHAPTER 21

Bobby quickly settled in to his new digs. He liked living alone and being responsible for his own comings and goings. Most of all, as Lucia was soon to discover, he was happy to be out from under what he considered to be the dark cloud of parental supervision.

The day after he moved in to his condo, Lucia called her son to remind him of a few things that every new homeowner needs to keep in mind, especially one who has never been on his own before.

"Mom," Bobby said at one point, his voice calm and matter-of-fact, "please don't call me often. I'm not a child, I'm an adult. I can take care of myself. I *want* to take care of myself. But I can't do much of anything if you and Dad are on my case every hour of every day."

"Of course, you can take care of yourself," Lucia said. "I'm just trying to help."

As she hung up, she felt gutted. Her mind had told her that this was how it would be after Bobby moved out of her home, but her heart could not yet accept it. She was not ready for it.

At first blush, to both Bobby and his parents, Bobby had what he wanted the most: independence. But there was more to it than that. To be truly independent and to contribute to society, Bobby also needed to earn a living. He needed a job. Without it he would still have to rely on his parents' goodwill and purse strings, and while he knew that they would never leave him high and dry, being forced to rely on them for his rent and living expenses ran contrary to everything he desired. He therefore was open to the notion of a job and even welcomed his mother's assistance in finding one.

Lucia scoured help-wanted announcements wherever she found them and called on her friends and professional contacts to help in the job search. After a month of casting their net into the waters, Bobby was able to land a position as a counselor in a counseling service office, serving adolescent children. The office was impressed with Bobby's story and with his bachelor's degree in family counseling from Texas Tech.

Although the first couple of days went well, the sense of excitement and satisfaction did not last long. Bobby had been on the job for only a week when Lucia received an angry call from the office manager demanding that Lucia come and get her son.

"What happened?" she asked.

"I'll tell you when you get here," the manager replied. "Just get here."

In his office, the manager informed Lucia that on the previous day, Bobby had been out with some boys and girls and, for no apparent reason, started screaming at them. The adolescents complained to their parents, who in turn complained to the office, demanding an explanation and clamoring for Bobby's head.

"They want to know why I allowed their children to be left alone with someone who has a mental problem," he said. "What do you suggest I tell them?"

The Bakirs and Hurs, deep-rooted friends

Best Diva friends of thirty-six years

Best Friends of thirty-six years enjoying an Alaskan cruises

SISTA Dee and her family with Hurs

Friends celebrating Julie's recovery!

Friend Ed Martin's big award day

Kinfolks Hans and Hurs

With close friends - Hawaiian cruise

Best Friends Shirley & Bob's
50th Wedding Anniversary

Annual Christmas portrait for our
decades-old movie group

## LOVEBIRDS JOHN & LUCIA

# LAST BUSINESS - ANTI-AGING SKINCARE REGIME

Derma-Lucia Skinceuticals Pre-Launch

# CIVIC, CHARITY, AND FUNDRAISING

Chair of TACC-Gala Night

Founder of Sister City Austin - Korea with Mayoral International Task Force

2013 Texas Asian Foundation Scholarship Reception

Congressman Doggett honoring TACC Board members

Lucia represented the United States as Miss NY of Korea

Lucia with Austin Mayor Kirk Watson - the International Task Force at Samsung reception

Lucia as founder of TAF with scholarship winners

Special Friends of over thirty-five years on charity event night

Judge Lucia with the Pacific Pageant princess

Special Needy Gift
fundraiser of Christmas,
2018

Lucia and TAF Board and
scholarship winners

TAF - Tsunami Fundraising
event at Lucia's home

## Texas Asian Foundation
### With the *Texas Asian Chamber of Commerce*

## Central Texas Wildfire Fundraising

Photo from EcoPoint, Inc. http://paintingdenver.net/blog/uncategorized/bastrop-county-raging-fire-photos/

On September 5, 2011, wildfires raged in Bastrop, Spicewood, Steiner Ranch and Pflugerville, destroying homes, property and devastating the lives for thousands in the Central Texas area.

*The Texas Asian Foundation (TAF), an affiliate of Texas Asian Chamber of Commerce (TACC), is a 501(c) 3 organization. Contributions to TAF are tax-deductible.*

The Texas Asian Foundation (TAF) held a fundraising dinner on September 16 to raise funds for the Central Texas wildfire victims. The fundraising effort continues online and future events are planned. Donate through TAF and 100 percent of your donation will reach those who need it most.

FOR MORE DETAILS, CONTACT LUCIA HUR- TACC@TXASIANCHAMBER.ORG

When Lucia had no immediate answer, the manager said, "It doesn't matter. Your son is not qualified to be a family counselor. He is no longer welcome here. Take him home."

Lucia had no choice but to comply. On the drive back to Bobby's condo, his mother asked him why he felt compelled to act so inappropriately toward the children.

Bobby shrugged. "They were acting up, Mom," he said. "You know how it is. They were making fun of each other and they were making fun of me. I was just trying to straighten them out."

Lucia suspected that her son was telling the truth. He may have many shortcomings, but she wondered if the manager should have been more understanding toward Bobby. But it was too late to do much about it, beyond allowing the incident to serve as a lesson for Bobby about how to better react to foolish and hurtful behavior.

Soon Bobby landed another counseling job, and it, too, started out well. Bobby seemed to be adapting well to the work schedule, and he was making decent money. Of far greater significance in the minds of his parents, Bobby was contributing something meaningful to society, something they had always stressed was of primary importance to any individual in any job.

Three weeks later, buoyed by what seemed a positive fresh start for Bobby, Lucia booked a flight to Nashville, Tennessee, to attend an industrial chemical convention. Two days after she arrived there, her cell phone rang, and a voice screamed at her, "Come take your son away right now!"

Lucia felt her stomach lurch. "Who is this?"

The man identified himself as Sam, the director of the organization Bobby worked for.

Lucia willed her voice to remain calm. "Please tell me what happened, Sam."

"I'll tell you what happened, Mrs. Hur," the man spat, "when you get here. Come right now!"

"I can't come right now. I'm in Nashville on business. I'll come tomorrow."

"What is it about the words 'right now' that you don't understand?" Sam shot back. It was as though he had not heard a word of Lucia's explanation.

"Listen," he added when Lucia failed to respond for a moment, "the client in question is about to sue us. By 'us' I mean you and me both. If you don't call the client and apologize, we're in deep trouble!"

Lucia drew a heavy sigh. "All right, Sam, I'll take care of it."

"You damn well better!"

On the way to the airport, Lucia called the client and promised to meet with her at nine the next morning. She then called Sam to tell him of the appointment. He seemed somewhat mollified.

When Lucia arrived in Austin, she drove straight home without stopping at Bobby's condo. She knew he was home; he had taken a cab from work. But she decided it was best to hear the client's side of the story first. She would then know how best to confront her son.

"What happened?" Lucia asked the pretty, stylish, thirty-something brunette whose name was Nancy. They had just sat down alone together in a private office.

Nancy explained her side of the story. She had come into the mental health offices, where Bobby worked, feeling very sad and seeking help. Bobby was assigned to her case and began by asking her what she was going through and how he could help her. So far, nothing out of the ordinary. He then started asking questions of a personal nature that made her uncomfortable. When she tried to steer the conversation back to the matter at hand, Bobby got up, closed the door, and said to her, with his hand on her shoulder, "Tell me everything. I want to know everything about you." He moved to block the door, thus providing her no exit. That was when she forced her way out of the room and later filed a complaint with the director's office.

As Lucia listened intently to Nancy's explanation, a mental image formed. Bobby had long been in the habit of closing the door behind him wherever he was, even when he was at home. Nancy may have seen that as a threatening gesture, but Lucia did not. In addition, to her mind, every other allegation made by Nancy could also be explained. None of them seemed to have much merit.

"I believe you misunderstood both my son and the situation, Nancy," Lucia said. "My son may be naïve, but he's not a bad person. Years ago, he was in a terrible car accident and suffered damage to his brain. But I can assure you he meant no harm to you."

"So, your son has a mental problem?" Nancy said. She cast Lucia a look of utter disbelief. "I was given counseling by a mentally challenged person? Is that what you are telling me?"

"No, that's not what I'm telling you," Lucia shot back. "What I am telling you is that Bobby went through a very difficult time, and he is now fully recovered. He graduated with a degree in family counseling from Texas Tech."

There was more Lucia wanted to say but did not; judging from Nancy's demeanor, she had already made up her mind and did not appear open to reason or common sense. Because of Bobby's TBI, he did not know when enough was enough, or when to stop and self-correct. He could thus easily make a mistake such as this. But both Nancy and society at large are intolerant of such mistakes, however innocent they may be.

"Please listen to reason, Nancy," Lucia said. "Bobby graduated from college after being in a coma for three months and after going through years of rehabilitation. It was sheer hell for him, and for his father and me. His rehab continues to this very day and probably will for the rest of his life. But he knows what he's doing and he means no harm to you or to anyone else. What he lacks in understanding he makes up for in caring. If anyone is at fault, I am. Perhaps I pushed him into work too quickly. Don't condemn him for that. Please forgive him!"

Nancy shook her head, more in frustration than bitterness. "Don't you think you should send a mental patient to a hospital rather than put him to work?" she asked. "It makes no sense to me, whatever issues he has overcome in the past."

She said no more. The conversation was over, and Lucia felt instinctively that Bobby would be fired regardless of how unfair Nancy's classification of Bobby as a "mental patient" was. Lucia understood that once again there would be no reprieve for her son. He had been found guilty in the eyes of an individual who served as judge and jury of Bobby's fate.

Lucia made her exit as soon as propriety allowed and rushed to her car to call Bobby. When she shared with Bobby the gist of her conversation with Nancy, Bobby hotly denied doing anything wrong.

"Bobby, listen to me!" Lucia said as she negotiated the streets. "This kind of thing has happened before and it will likely happen again, because you go too far. You ask for too much. As I have told you many times before, you have to learn when you need to stop doing what you're doing and leave it behind you. And you have to learn what is considered professional behavior. It's not what you think it is; it's what society says it is. You ignore that simple truth at your peril."

"You say that only because you don't understand counseling," Bobby retorted. "A counselor has to hear all the facts of the case. Otherwise he can't offer valid counseling. That's pretty basic, don't you think?"

Lucia agreed. It was *very* basic. Anger surged through her at the thought of how unforgiving society can be toward handicapped individuals, no matter their character or intention, or how diligently they are struggling to get back into society. For all the platitudes she had just delivered, her son remained a victim of cruel circumstance.

Soon after Bobby was fired, Lucia managed to arrange several volunteer counseling jobs. Her intent was to give Bobby some meaningful work experience in a discipline he understood, with the hope that he could leverage such experience to land a steady job. But these initiatives, too, failed. Something in Bobby's personality prevented him from listening patiently and cogently to people's problems, which prevented him from being an effective counselor. In other words, he was unable to apply classroom theory to "live" situations at work. Lucia suspected it was a combination of his temper and his tendency to get overly emotional, or overly involved.

Lucia was not about to give up on her son's work career, however. While counseling jobs may not have been in the cards at the moment, surely there were other kinds of jobs Bobby could do. Office administration came to mind. As fate would have it, soon thereafter there was a job opening for an administrative clerk at the Texas Department of Criminal Justice. They were seeking someone to read profiles, and then categorize and organize documents within each file. The position seemed ideal, since the Texas state government is required to hire a certain percentage of handicapped people.

When she broached the subject with Bobby, Bobby became angry, claiming he was overqualified for the job and that it was therefore beneath him. But Lucia persuaded him to apply by extolling the benefits of different work experiences, and Bobby got the job.

On the morning of his first day, Lucia said to him, "Bobby, do not, under any conditions, give flowers to a female employee. Do not write poems for them either. Remember: You are now working for the government of Texas. You must always conduct yourself like a gentleman and be on your best behavior. Okay?"

"Okay," he agreed.

The days rolled into weeks, the weeks into months, and the months into a full year without incident. Bobby seemed very content in his work, and from what his parents could tell, his employers were pleased with his performance. As each month blended into the next, John and Lucia breathed a little easier. With the one-year anniversary of Bobby's start date, they felt downright giddy. They began to earnestly believe that their ship had come in. More to the point, that Bobby's ship had come in.

But they were wrong. Bobby's ship was in fact heading for the rocks.

# CHAPTER 22

One day out of the blue, Lucia received a call from Bobby's boss, who informed her that her son had been arrested.

"Arrested?" Lucia gasped. "On what charge?"

"Possession of marijuana."

"*What?*"

A minute after placing a call to John, Lucia was in her car, heading downtown to the sheriff's station at the Texas Department of Criminal Justice, where Bobby was being held. When she was allowed into the retention area and saw him sitting there dejectedly, she rushed up to him.

"Is it true, Bobby?" she asked him. "Is it true what they say?"

Bobby shook his head.

"No, Mom, it's not true," he said adamantly. "I did not smoke marijuana! I wanted to give my urine specimen but nothing is coming out. I swear it."

"Well, that's a relief!" Lucia let out a long sigh and sat down next to her son. Bobby may have acquired unsettling habits and characteristics since the accident, but, to her knowledge, he had never lied to her about matters of this importance. "So, what happened?"

"Nothing happened. I just went outside for a smoke."

"Was anyone with you? Did you see anyone there? Someone who can corroborate your story?"

"Just a coworker who asked me for a light. So, I gave him one."

"Do you know this coworker?"

"I know who he is," Bobby said. "I don't hang around with him or anyone in his crowd. They all hate my guts. You know why."

Lucia did know why. It was not only his handicap that differentiated Bobby from his coworkers, it was also his arrogance and demeanor. *Yes*, Lucia thought, *Bobby does like to show off.* For better or worse, that had been part of his nature long before the accident. He would tell his co-workers—most of whom came from poor, hard-working families—that he had gone to college and earned a degree, and that his parents were wealthy. His intimation in such encounters was that he was better than them. John and Lucia had always disapproved of such behavior and always would. But that was hardly the point at the moment.

"And you believe this coworker planted the marijuana on you?" Lucia said. "He slipped it into your pocket when he asked you for a light?"

"I not only believe it, Mom, I know it. I was set up."

Lucia could see it all in her mind's eye. The coworker slipped a small package of marijuana into Bobby's coat pocket—there had been a cold snap in Texas and everyone was wearing a light overcoat—and had then reported to Bobby's boss that Bobby was smoking marijuana in the outdoor smoking area. When Bobby returned to his office, he was greeted by a sheriff, who searched Bobby's clothing. He found the package of marijuana and Bobby was arrested. The Texas Department of Criminal Justice has a zero-tolerance rule regarding marijuana. The fact that the quantity was small did not matter. All that mattered was possession. For that, he was charged with a felony. As Lucia was to discover, while possession of marijuana was not considered a criminal act in other parts of Texas, it was considered a criminal act on the campus of the state's Department of Criminal Justice.

What could they do? The first step was to convince the sheriff that since Bobby was no threat to society, and had no past history of imprisonment, he should be allowed to return home to await further developments. The sheriff agreed. Beyond that, Lucia had no clue. She knew enough of Texas law that she somehow had to get Bobby's arrest stricken from the record. If it was not, Bobby would encounter many unpleasant challenges in the future, such as landing any sort of job anywhere. The fact that he had been charged while working for a state agency compounded the problem and the potential consequences. But for the moment all they could do was wait to see what happened next.

What they saw, a few days later, was a subpoena to appear in Texas Department of Criminal Justice court in three weeks. The letter went on to specify that Bobby was allowed to be accompanied by one person and one person only.

At first blush it seemed logical that the one person to accompany Bobby would be the family lawyer. That individual had already been acquainted with the facts of the case and was standing by to serve. In discussions with John and close friends, however, it was decided that Bobby's case could not be won by a legal strategy. The best they could hope for from a lawyer, John argued, was a reduced sentence.

Lucia's friend Bob, whom she respected highly, thought the same.

"You have to appeal to their emotions," he said, "and you have to appeal to them as the mother who saved her child's life by bringing him back from the abyss to serve society in the best way he knows how. No one else can do that the way you can, for the simple reason that you are the one who did it."

Lucia agreed. But she was deathly afraid of knowing that the fate of her son rested on her. She started having cold sweats and nightmarish visions of Bobby behind iron bars. The insomnia that had been daunting her for years was now reinforced by countless hours devoted to preparing for battle. After she would finally fall asleep, she often awoke with a start from what she swore was the sound of voices shrieking at her.

So, it was decided that Lucia would accompany her son to the Texas Department of Criminal Justice's internal court system. In preparation, she gathered what documents she could to support Bobby's case, such as his hospital records, his progress in rehabilitation, his diploma from Texas Tech, and the self-published book of poems he had written. She also crafted a detailed chronology involving who, what, when, and where from the day of the accident to the present day. It was a grueling exercise, but she felt it might be put to good use. She also did extensive research into the legal underpinnings of a case such as Bobby's.

The court hearing was set for nine o'clock on a Thursday morning. Lucia and Bobby were in the waiting area before eight o'clock. When a court attendant summoned them in, Lucia saw the four chief administrators—for the purposes of the department's court system, these were essentially the judges—seated at a large raised table on a platform. They were looking down at her and her son as they each took a seat at a table positioned in front of the slightly raised dais. From the door leading in and out of the court, a sheriff watched the proceedings.

The judges allowed Lucia to speak on behalf of her son. Although they knew who she was, after she rose to her feet, she introduced herself and thanked each judge in turn for the opportunity to address the court. Then she opened her defense by pointing out that the arresting officer could not obtain either a urine or blood test at the time of the arrest. A judge replied that such a fact was immaterial to the case. Possession alone was sufficient cause for Bobby to be charged with a felony. Lucia then launched into the heart of her defense.

"Your Honors," she said in measured tones, "I request with respect that you carefully consider the historical context for the case before you. My son Bobby"—she rested her hand on the shoulder of the young man sitting beside her, dressed in suit and tie— "was involved in a terrible automobile accident that sent him into a deep coma and nearly claimed his life. His doctors in Lubbock all but gave up on him. They told my husband and me that even if by some miracle he came out of the coma, he would, in all likelihood, live out his life in a vegetative state.

"But, Your Honors, miracles do happen. I stand before you as an eyewitness to a miracle. I watched my son not only emerge from the coma after three months, I saw him make progress every day with each stumbling step he managed to take, with each tortured word he was able to force out. It was no easy thing, Your Honors. I can assure you of that. My husband and I had a lifetime's worth of worries and despair and tears as we watched our son fight for his life, and then for his rightful place in society. Ultimately, he was able to relearn a great deal and was accepted at Austin Community College and then at Texas Tech, where he earned a bachelor's degree in family counseling. As far as we know, no one suffering from a severe traumatic brain injury has ever gone back to college to finish his degree.

"Yes, he has made mistakes. I can't deny that. Nor can he. But understand, Your Honors, traumatic brain injury, which is what Bobby suffered as a result of the accident, has unpleasant consequences. TBI makes people act in ways they would never have acted otherwise. It makes them say things that they would not otherwise say. And it makes it hard for Bobby to make friends, since what he does and what he says unintentionally hurts other people's feelings. But the real tragedy of all of this is the simple fact that because his behavior seems odd or out of control, society has rejected Bobby. It wants nothing to do with him. He is not the perpetrator of what has happened. He is the victim."

Lucia paused to stare intently at each judge in turn.

"You have the facts before you, Your Honors," she went on. "You have heard my words and you have read the reports and other materials I have sent you. Do you not agree in your hearts that my son deserves another chance? Please, Your Honors, give him that chance. I implore you. Bobby did not make a good impression on his coworkers. He was boastful of his hard-earned degree and behaved childishly with his privileges. I am not here to point fingers at his coworkers, but merely to state that it is some misconception and misunderstanding that might have led to this chaotic mess."

As Lucia sat down, she chanced a glance at Bobby. He nodded at his mother, unable to hide the glint of tears in his eyes. Half an hour later the verdict came down. Two judges voted to acquit; the two others voted not to acquit. Since it was a split decision, Lucia was informed, a higher judge would have to make the ruling on the next appeal date. In the meantime, Bobby would have to be confined to jail. That harsh ruling was confirmed by the hard bang of a gavel.

As the four judges got up to leave and the court sheriff walked over to take Bobby away, Lucia collapsed in a near faint onto the floor, clinging to her son for dear life. She was at the point of a nervous breakdown as her world closed in around her.

"*Please* don't do this!" Lucia begged the sheriff, beside herself with grief. She fell to her knees. She pulled and tugged the sheriff's pants from her kneeling position on the floor, beseeching him with every fiber of her being. Her words came fast and furiously. "Please don't put my son in jail. He is not a criminal. Don't make him live like one! He almost died in that accident. Can't you understand? Can't you feel my pain? Don't you have children of your own? Would you send one of them to jail? *Please* show some compassion and help me!"

The sheriff had been watching and listening to Lucia since she came into the courtroom. When she went silent, weeping into the hands she held to her face, he came to her, put a hand on her arm, and helped her to her feet.

"I do have a son," he said to her. "He's nineteen. And I can tell you I have never seen anything like this in my thirty years of service."

Lucia looked at the sheriff with a crazed expression. She thought she saw tears in his eyes, but dismissed them as a mirage.

"Can you help me?" she implored him.

"I don't know," the sheriff said. "I'll see what I can do. You and your son wait here."

Lucia had no idea how long the sheriff was gone. The courtroom was deathly quiet, empty but for Lucia and Bobby, neither of whom spoke, each lost in thought. It was as though a single word spoken between them might upset the gods of mercy. At length, the door creaked open and the sheriff walked back in.

Lucia gazed at him through watery eyes, her heart thumping and her insides roiling.

He took in her gaze and stepped in close, as if in confidence.

"I talked to the two judges who found your son guilty," he said sotto voce, "and I convinced them to let him go free." He held up a square of paper. "It's all here in the release form signed by all four judges."

Lucia's mouth went wide, as if she were about to shout something. But no sound came out. She then buried her face in her hands and wept. Bobby put a comforting hand on her back.

"However," the sheriff went on, his voice firm, his tone strict, "as this form specifies, your son may never again work for a campus or location of a TDCJ agency. In addition, if anything like this incident happens again, the court will not be as forgiving. Your son will be in serious trouble. All four judges are quite clear on this point. Do you understand?"

"Yes! Yes! I understand!" Lucia sobbed. "I understand." She lifted her gaze to meet his. "Thank you, officer! Thank you for saving my son! We will never forget your extraordinary kindness today. Never!"

The sheriff nodded his understanding. He looked at Bobby. "You understand all that I just told your mother, son?"

"Yes, sir, I do," Bobby replied. He then added from the heart, "Thank you, sir. I will never forget what happened here today."

"See that you don't." The sheriff stared at them for several moments more before raising his right hand as if in benediction.

"God bless you both," he said. He turned and walked out of the courtroom, closing the door softly behind him.

# CHAPTER 23

After the salvation bestowed upon the Hur family by the sheriff of the court, Lucia decided not to pursue or even advocate another job opportunity for Bobby, at least not at this stage. It was bad enough that Bobby had been terminated from previous jobs for reasons that were questionable at best; it was quite another to be found guilty and incarcerated for a crime he did not commit. Lucia and John finally came to terms with the reality that society has neither the room nor the stomach to accommodate someone like Bobby, with his poor communication, social skills, slurred speech, and pronounced limp.

It was a vicious cycle. Since Bobby could not interact in what was perceived by others as a normal and, therefore, acceptable manner, he was often left to his own devices. His way of compensating for this deficiency was to act in a condescending manner, as if he were somehow superior to everyone else. That attitude grated on people, causing them to draw further away, which exacerbated the situation. That sort of reaction served only to confirm in Bobby's mind his sense of superiority—and as a result, his sense of isolation from society at large.

Since the accident there had been no breaking of the cycle. Around and around it went, rehab session after rehab session, job after job, any sort of event that demanded Bobby's participation. Nothing that Lucia and John did or said seemed to matter.

One day, Peter came to visit his parents. He brought with him his wife and two young children, who, like most children their age, could be both angelic and impish almost in the same breath. That first evening, as his wife was tucking her young ones into bed, Peter seized a few minutes alone with his mother.

"Mom," he said, "I must ask you, please, to give more thought to me and my family. Since the accident, it has been all about Bobby. I realize you and Dad have been acting out of love and you've had a lot on your mind—I realize a lot of things these days that I didn't understand before—but I remind you that you have another son who has often felt like a forgotten soul these past few years. I also remind you that you have a daughter-in-law and two grandchildren who need you, too. It's not just about me."

Lucia looked hard at her older son.

"I'm sorry if you feel I've neglected you, Peter," she said. "That certainly was not my intention, nor Dad's. But may I remind you, in turn, that we have often invited you and your family down here to Austin or somewhere else to celebrate a family event or just to spend time together. Aside from those trips to Cancun, Vegas, and Orlando, how many times did you accept those invitations?"

Peter nodded. "I can accept my responsibility," he said in a mature tone that Lucia had rarely heard from him before. "I just felt that if I came down here, it would still be just about Bobby. I wouldn't get much attention. So, I figured, what was the point?"

"I see," Lucia said. "And what is your point this evening? What do you want me to do?"

"I want you to stop doing what you're doing."

"Stop doing what?"

"Money, time, interference, forcing your agenda, overprotection, everything. Stop it all. Dad and I are your family, too. Spend time with your grandchildren. Enjoy them. Play with them. Get some time off with Dad. You two go somewhere by yourselves. You need some alone time together. Take it. Enjoy it. Live it up even for a little while. God knows you two have earned it."

Their eyes locked. Lucia set her jaw. "I see. And would you then be prepared to carry my load? Even for a little while?"

Peter dropped his gaze. "You know what I mean, Mom," he said quietly.

"I do, Peter," Lucia said, her features softening. "I do know what you mean. Tell me, do you think I treat Bobby like a child?"

Peter nodded. "I do, Mom. Bobby is not a handicapped person. But you treat him like one by doing everything for him. Besides, he has become quite the manipulator, more so now than at any other time since the accident."

Although Peter's words resonated with her, they did little to improve relations between him and Bobby. During Peter's visit home, Bobby met a girl whom Peter immediately disliked. He informed Bobby that if he brought that girl home for dinner, as he had said he would, then Peter and his family would return to Lubbock.

"If you won't let me bring her, I won't show up either," was Bobby's response.

It broke Lucia's heart to hear her sons argue that way. She and John had always pursued family harmony, particularly between their two sons. It had been that way before the accident—they had been not only brothers but best friends, at least until Bobby started playing football in high school. Since they were young boys, Bobby had been trying to find his own identity outside of his older brother's realm. But since the accident, their relationship had turned sour. Lucia understood why, but she felt powerless to change things. Too much water had flowed over the dam and under the bridge.

In years gone by, if there had been a need to mend hurt feelings or attend to frayed emotions within the family, Lucia would have recommended a family vacation to an exotic locale. Such vacations were rare—there was the expense to consider, and it was often difficult to find a week or two that suited everybody—but they were usually purposeful and meaningful events.

That had not been the case with the trip to Cancun.

A few years after Bobby left the hospital and started to walk again, Lucia proposed a family vacation in Cancun to celebrate life and to allow the family to bond after the years of hardship and despair. All the elements were in place: a week's stay at a classy resort near the beach; a hot, yellow sun; palm fronds rustling in the soft sea breezes; the inviting turquoise waters of the Gulf of Mexico.

The reality turned out to be quite different, however. Both John and Peter were skeptical that the dream could become a reality. Although Lucia had her share of misgivings and premonitions about the trip, she was determined to see it through.

The trouble began at airport security after they had checked in and received their boarding passes. Bobby was found in possession of a Swiss Army knife, an item he often carried on his person and an item his father had warned him about before leaving for the airport. "Put it in your check-through bag," he warned his son, but Bobby had failed to heed his advice.

"You are not allowed on the plane with a knife," the security officer informed Bobby. "I have no choice but to confiscate it."

When the officer moved to take the knife away from Bobby, Bobby went berserk. He attacked the officer, screaming, "Give my knife back to me! You can't take it away from me!" The airport police came running as John and Peter tried to restrain Bobby and Lucia explained to anyone who would listen that her son was a victim of severe brain damage and meant no harm to anyone. But Bobby did not calm down, even when a more senior security officer told Bobby that they would hold the knife for him and that he could claim it on his return to the States. Lucia had to beg the security officer to give the knife to the pilot so that Bobby could retrieve it once they landed in Cancun. This was pre-9/11; airport security was much more accommodating.

As it turned out, that unpleasant incident marked only the beginning. Once they arrived at the hotel, unpacked, and got out into the open air, conflict seemed to follow them wherever they went. Peter wanted to go jet skiing, and because he did, so did Bobby. But Lucia put a stop to that notion.

"You can't go jet skiing, Bobby," she told her son.

"Why not?" Bobby fired back. "I can do it."

"No, you can't," John said. "Think about it. You may be walking well enough, but your sense of balance is nowhere near what it should be. Jet skiing demands good and steady balance."

"I said I can do it, Dad!"

"And I said you can't. It's too dangerous!"

A compromise was finally reached that calmed the waters: the boys would ride a two-seater jet ski. But Peter's adventurous spirit was dampened, and Bobby remained resentful.

And so, it went, that day and into the next, when Bobby announced he was going to ride a horse on his own.

"No, Bobby," his mother said. "You can't do those kinds of things. Not yet. You may be able to someday, but not today. Remember what happened to Christopher Reeve when he fell off a horse? The same thing could happen to you."

"You are not human!" Bobby screamed at her. In response, as yet another compromise, Lucia was able to secure an older, tame donkey that Bobby could ride on his own.

As it had the previous day, his surly response caused people to stare and little children to giggle. When Peter wanted to play the Mexican hockey game riding on the donkey, Bobby also wanted to play riding the donkey. That conflict led to more tantrums, more explosions.

Two days later, after several such incidents, Peter had had enough.

"I want to go home, Mom," he announced. "This dream vacation has turned into a nightmare."

To Peter's surprise, his words did not cause his mother to flinch or become angry. Instead, they seemed to draw the wind out of her sails. Her normally vibrant demeanor went limp, and she slowly exhaled a long breath.

"I know how you feel, Peter," she said quietly. "I am so very tired, and I want to go home, too. But if you leave, we all leave. How sad would that be? We may never again have a vacation together. Leaving now before the week is up would be like giving up on our family. Is that what you want? Do you really want your mother to be so miserable?"

Peter's hard features softened. He sat down beside his mother and took her hand in his. That simple gesture caused Lucia to lean into him and burst into tears.

"I have failed you, Peter," she said through tears. "I've failed you and I am so sorry."

Peter embraced her and held her close.

"You have not failed me, Mom," he said, from the heart. "You've failed yourself. Since Bobby's accident, you've given up on your life and the life of the family." When Lucia moved to respond, Peter held her tighter. "I'm sorry, Mom. I didn't mean that. And I didn't really mean it when I said I wanted to leave. It's just that, in the past, every time I saw you, I got angry. I thought you didn't want me around. I thought my being around you and Dad just made things harder for you. I can't seem to help my brother. He makes me so angry. We fight all the time, especially when he's manipulative and tries to get his own way. Bobby thinks he has the worst possible fate and that he's the only one who has ever experienced pain. That's why I stayed away. That's why I didn't come to visit you and Dad. It hurt too much. Truth is, I didn't realize what you were going through. I didn't realize how challenging your life had become. I didn't know what you were going through, every day. Now I know."

Peter released his grip. Lucia drew away reluctantly.

"Thank you for saying that, Peter," she said. "It means everything to me." She swiped at her tears with her forearm. "You see, I couldn't give up on Bobby. I just couldn't. Whatever it took. I still feel that way. But it doesn't mean I stopped loving you. That could never happen. If I hurt you as a consequence of what I did, I am so very, very sorry. You are my son, and I love you. Someday you'll understand all of this better. Someday you'll be a father and you'll realize that parents tend to gravitate toward the child who, for whatever reason, needs the most attention. This is not done by choice. This is done by necessity. Do not think for a moment that just because we spend so much more time on Bobby that we love you any less."

"I love you, too, Mom," Peter said, in a hot rush of tears.

When the week ended and the family made preparations to return to Austin, Lucia repacked her belongings with mixed feelings. She was keen to return to a place one beloved son called home, but she was also sad to leave a place where the depth of her love for her other son had been reconfirmed.

# CHAPTER 24

Several months later, Lucia received a call from her doctor's office reminding her of her annual mammogram. She had postponed the appointment several times due to her demanding schedule, but this time she reluctantly agreed. During the examination her radiologist found some questionable lesions on her breast tissue. They kept taking more pictures of the scans for better resolution.

"Have you noticed anything unusual about your breasts before today?" the doctor asked her.

When he handed her a box of tissues, Lucia felt the first inkling of nausea.

"Sorry, Doctor," she said. "I've been neglecting the self-examinations I should have been doing. What have you found?"

"Well, it's probably nothing, but I'd still like to have it checked out. That will put your mind at rest, as well as mine."

Further ultrasound tests were scheduled, and the results were not good. Lucia was urgently escorted to see a surgeon that same day. The female surgeon calmly informed her that she should have a small lumpectomy, a surgery in which only the tumor and some surrounding tissue are removed to determine if the tumor is benign or malignant.

Lucia therefore had the surgery to get the job done, then refused to think much more about it. She was so confident of good results that the next day she rushed off to a national convention in New Jersey. She had just left the airport and was heading for the convention center when she received the call from her surgeon: the results were in, and they were not good. The surgeon urged her to schedule another surgery as soon as possible, because she believed the tumor was cancerous.

"But I can't go back," Lucia insisted. "I'm at a conference in New Jersey. It's for a new formula I'm developing for the launch of my new business. I can't miss it."

"Cancer tends not to be overly concerned with one's schedule," the doctor said, not unkindly.

Lucia thanked the doctor and promised to be back in touch the next day.

In the meantime, Lucia's brother Augustine, the chairman at Weill Cornell in New York City, tried to reach Lucia on the convention floor. Unbeknownst to Lucia, John had called Augustine and informed him of the recent developments. Augustine, not fully convinced that his sister had received the correct diagnosis, had called Lucia's surgeon to request that the biopsy specimen be overnighted to him for further analysis.

When he got the results, he was stunned. It was worse than he had been led to believe. There was no doubt about it: the diagnosis was cancer.

"Come to New York," Augustine told his sister. "Come immediately. I'll make an appointment for you at Weill Cornell, and all the other necessary arrangements. Weill Cornell is one of the top cancer centers in the world. You'll be in excellent hands here."

Lucia had little choice but to do as she was told. Both her husband and her brother were insisting that she get to Weill Cornell as soon as possible. She had no will—and was too numb—to resist. She could not fathom what was happening to her. She was too dumbfounded to feel anything at all. She was going through the motions as though she were a robot.

That very afternoon she suffered through another round of dignity-defying tests that served only to confirm breast cancer. The tests also confirmed that the cancer had likely not metastasized.

"That's the good news, Lucia," Augustine said when he delivered the test results in his office. He smiled down at her as she sat there looking up at him.

Despite the emotions of the moment, she could not help feeling a surge of pride: Augustine looked so confident and helpful and handsome, with such caring, kind eyes and a reassuring bedside manner. The very image of their father as a younger man. A doctor that any hospital would wish to show off.

"We have every reason to have hope," he continued. "But surgery will be required. The question is, do you want to have the surgery here in New York or at the Anderson Cancer Center in Houston?"

Lucia shook her head. It was all too much. This was not a business decision; this was a life-and-death decision.

"What do you recommend?" she asked him.

"Here, of course," Augustine replied. "But the choice is yours, since I can also arrange the best team of doctors down in Houston."

Lucia knew that Augustine, as the chairman of Weill Cornell, had the reputation and the clout to do just about anything in the medical field.

"You and I will talk again tomorrow," he added. "We need to move on this as soon as possible."

When Lucia put the question to John, he was upset that she was even considering Houston.

"But if I have the surgery in Houston," Lucia pointed out, "I'll be near you and our boys. Anderson is an excellent hospital, and plus, all the post-op trips will be more convenient."

"What are you thinking?" John demanded. "In New York your brother will put together the best team of doctors available anywhere. You can't find a better hospital than Weill Cornell. And I'll stay there with you. No, you will have your surgery in New York, and that's final!"

"Okay, John," Lucia said. "Augustine told me the surgery will be scheduled within the week if I decide to have it done here. I'll explain things to Peter and Bobby when I'm home."

The next several days, back in Austin, were difficult ones for Lucia. Her world had suddenly turned upside down, and she had a myriad of details to attend to before the return trip to New York. Addressing domestic and company logistics was one thing; addressing family dynamics and emotions turned out to be quite another.

Because Peter lived in Lubbock, Lucia had to tell him her news by phone. Normally a pragmatic man, Peter reacted with a greater intensity of feeling than Lucia could have imagined. He wanted to come to Austin immediately with his family, but Lucia talked him out of it.

"Your Uncle Augustine," she told him, "is highly confident that the surgery will be a complete success. There is no need to worry. Besides," she added, "I'll be in touch by phone on a daily basis."

Bobby's response to the news was more enigmatic. He had very little to say, despite the same upbeat delivery Lucia had used with Peter. He merely nodded when Lucia asked him if he understood what she was telling him. When she leaned in to embrace him, Bobby hugged her back with a strength Lucia had until now experienced only in the heat of his anger. That afternoon, she left her son's apartment with a heavy heart. She knew instinctively that Bobby felt the same as she did, and that knowledge warmed her soul. She would beat this cancer, she pronounced to her inner depths. If Bobby could survive and prosper after what he had had to endure, she could, too. By God, she would beat this!

Two days before Lucia and John were to leave for New York, Lucia received a call from a hospital in Los Angeles. Her father, she was informed, had been taken there.

"What does he have?" Lucia asked.

"Walking pneumonia," the spokesman responded. "It's quite serious, and at his age there is considerable risk."

"I see," Lucia said. "Please tell my father I will be there tomorrow."

"He will be pleased to hear that, I can assure you."

John, however, was not pleased. Nor were her brother and the other doctors at Weill Cornell.

"It could be risky for you to travel such a long distance in your condition," Augustine told her on the phone. "I love our father, too, but you can see him after the surgery. It's what he would want. In fact, he would insist on it. I'll do everything I can to get out to L.A. to see him myself. But for the moment, my first concern is you. You could get overtired and decrease your immune system on such a long trip. I mean, going to the West Coast and then back to the East Coast for surgery? Please reconsider."

John knew his wife would not reconsider no matter how much he might plead. They had lived with each other long enough to be well aware of the other's habits, proclivities, and nuances. Arguing would be pointless. Besides, he understood the love underlying Lucia's decision. Her father was eighty-five years old, and if anything happened before she could visit with him, Lucia would never forgive herself, whatever the circumstances. She decided, therefore, to fly to Los Angeles from Austin and spend one day and night with her father. Her surgery would be delayed by four days.

On the flight to Los Angeles Lucia basked in a lifetime of memories: memories of her childhood in Korea and then Singapore; memories of her father and mother and siblings; memories of her battles to save Bobby's life and reclaim his future; memories of all the little words, smiles, and attentions John had given her over their years of living and loving together. She also felt the dread of what was to come: a surgery that would remove her breast and claim yet another part of her body that defined her femininity, as if the hysterectomy had not been enough.

At the hospital she was shocked by the apparition peering up at her from her father's bed. It had been more than a year since Lucia last saw him, and it had not been a kind year. He lay there weak and debilitated and shattered, a shadow of his former self.

"Dad," she choked, dropping to her knees and taking his gnarled hand in her own. His was a hand that had once performed the most intricate of surgeries, usually to a successful conclusion. Dr. Choi had saved many lives during his brilliant career. Now others were fighting to save his.

"Lucia, my dear daughter," he rasped. "How good of you to come."

"You knew I'd come," Lucia managed.

Her father smiled. "Yes, Lucia. I know you. I knew you would come." He gave her hand a weak squeeze.

Her father was too weak to talk much. Lucia sat next to him and started talking about his favorite topic: Augustine's accomplishments, as the only one of his children who had followed in the footsteps of this man who had dreamt that all his children would become successful physicians. He had not heard all the details about Augustine's path to Weill Cornell, and Lucia took delight in filling her father in. His eyes beamed with pride and tears trickled down his cheeks as he lay frail and helpless. By the time Lucia had to say goodbye to leave for New York, he had lost even more of his strength.

On the table by his bedside lay a copy of Bobby's self-published book of poetry, In the *Hur Ri Kean*. Judging by the dog-eared pages, he had been reading through it often, his attention probably drawn to what was perhaps his favorite of his grandson's poems.

"The Struggle in Life"
*Life will be his struggle,*
*Yeahhhhhh, he grows in exhaustion at the fight,*
*Yet, he will worship the silence of the everlasting thought,*
*Never will he surrender to the pain of the dwelling past,*
*Head held high, in the pride of courage.*
*He knows the perseverance that has been displayed before his spirit*
*by the soul of his champion that will sit on the throne.*
*He will be, the itinerant preacher,*
*Of strength, of wisdom, of faith,*
*Of the limitless vision, without the walls,*
*He will reach to eternity,*
*He will find the heart,*

*So full of love,*
*And devotion,*
*All of the questions,*
*Are answered,*
*He will understand and will not fight,*
*The unknown, the unseen.*
*All of this yearns to be accepted, not understood.*
*The fight will be in the soul, standing lost,*
*His courage will hold him firm.*

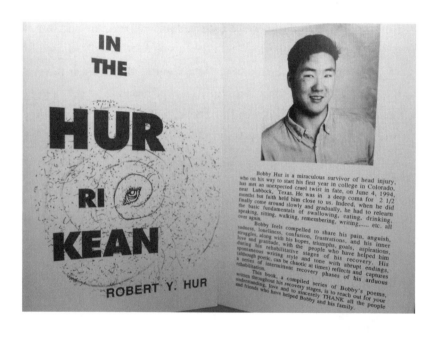

IN THE HUR RI KEAN

ROBERT Y. HUR

Bobby Hur is a miraculous survivor of head injury, who on his way to start his first year in college in Colorado, has met an unexpected cruel twist in fate, on June 4, 1994, near Lubbock, Texas. He was in a deep coma for 2 1/2 months but faith held him close to us. Indeed, when he did finally come around slowly and gradually, he had to relearn the basic fundamentals of swallowing, eating, drinking, speaking, sitting, walking, remembering, writing...... etc. all over again.

Bobby feels compelled to share his pain, anguish, sadness, loneliness, confusion, frustrations, and his inner struggles, along with his hopes, triumphs, goals, aspirations, love and gratitude, with the people who have helped him during his rehabilitative stages of his recovery. His spontaneous writing style and tone with abrupt endings, (although poetic, can be chaotic at times) reflects and captures a series of intermittent recovery phases of his arduous rehabilitation.

This book, a compiled series of Bobby's poems, written throughout his recovery stages, is to reach out for your understanding, love and to sincerely THANK all the people and friends who have helped Bobby and his family.

# CHAPTER 25

The next day, Lucia boarded a nonstop flight to New York. As planned, they went directly to Weill Cornell. The surgery went as scheduled and without a hitch. When Lucia emerged from the anesthesia, her vision was, at first, a bit blurry. She had to struggle to recall where she was and why she was there. One shadow stood by her bedside. She blinked, knowing in her heart who it was.

"John?"

She felt his lips on her forehead and the warmth of his hand on hers.

"Yes, honey, it's me," he said soothingly. "Welcome back."

"The operation…"

"Went extremely well. Augustine will be in shortly. He'll confirm what I just said. They're quite sure they got all the cancer. You're going to be just fine, honey. Just fine."

During their final conversation, Lucia's father had assured her that all would be fine, and that there is always hope. The thought of his words ignited a rush of fond remembrance. She raised her head to gaze around the room, and then glanced down at her chest. She slumped back onto the pillow. She could not believe that her right breast was completely gone. A complete mastectomy! *Did it really happen?* she wondered. She then noticed the tubes around her breast and the droplets of blood trickling down those tubes.

"Rest now, honey," John said. "You need to rest. I'll wake you when Augustine pays you a visit."

At her husband's bidding, Lucia slipped away into a blissful slumber. What seemed like moments later, she felt someone gently shake her shoulder and speak into her ear. She awoke with a start to see Augustine and the surgeon standing beside her hospital bed, smiling down at her, John behind them.

"Well, good afternoon, sleepyhead," Augustine said. "Nice of you to join us. What do you think this is, a spa where you can blob out all day?"

In spite of herself, Lucia smiled. But she said nothing in response.

"As I know John has told you," the surgeon added, "everything went as well as can be expected. As you're well aware, there are no guarantees in this business, but at the moment it certainly looks good."

"That's good to hear," Lucia said.

"Yes, it is. And it will come as no surprise to you, this husband of yours"—he glanced at John— "refused to leave this room the entire time you were in here. When we tried to get him to vamoose, he refused. We called hospital security, but he sent them packing. So, we decided to let him stay. A nurse brought in a cot for him."

Her gaze shifted to her husband.

"Thank you, John," she said softly.

He replied with a simple nod.

"Have you told Bobby?" Lucia asked him. "And Peter?"

"I've called them both every day. They are relieved to hear the good news, of course. But I must tell you, honey, that Bobby has been taking this very hard. He has been on the verge of tears several times in several conversations. He may have an odd way of showing it, but he loves you very much."

"I know he does," Lucia breathed. In the next breath she asked her brother when she would be discharged from the hospital.

"That depends on your recovery," Augustine said. "I suspect in a few days. But I want you to stay that long, at least, because we need to drain out all the residual blood from your mastectomy.

"I've arranged for you to stay at a post-care hotel next door while we continue to monitor you. You'll receive more detailed instruction on what you need to do on a daily basis, but the important things to remember are that you need to get as much rest as possible and that you need to increase your immune system. I'll be checking on you every day to make sure you are sticking with the program."

"Thank you, dear little brother!" she said. "And thanks for arranging my post-care treatments. Before going home, I want to fly to L.A. to see Dad one more time. He's not doing well, and I fear it may be the last time I see him."

"We'll discuss that," Augustine said.

Several days later, John took Lucia out of the post-care hotel for a walk in Central Park, which had become their daily exercise. Although it was often snowing, it was good for Lucia to walk around the park. Slowly, they would wind along the well-tended woodsy trails around the lake, keeping in sight the impressive facades of Central Park West.

Normally on these walks, Lucia did the talking and John the listening. Today it was the opposite, Lucia remaining deep in thought while John went on about his early days in New York with IBM. Eventually, after a significant lull in conversation, he broached the subject hanging over them both.

"Are you still determined to fly to L.A.?"

Lucia avoided his eyes when she responded.

"Yes, John, I am," she said. "I need to see my father again. Something tells me it could be the last time."

"You don't know that," John protested. "I don't think it's a good idea. You're still in recovery, and traveling such a long distance in your condition could be harmful to you. Can't you wait a little while?"

"No, hon. I'm afraid I can't wait."

John fell silent for a spell.

"Right, then," he said. "Let's go back to the hotel and book a flight to Los Angeles. I'll call the boys to tell them what we're doing."

Back in their room, Lucia received a call from John, her stepbrother from her dad's second marriage.

"Lucia," he said quietly, "your dad died a few minutes ago."

Lucia dropped her phone and cried out. "No, no, it cannot be!" she wailed. "Not my father. Not my poor, dear, wonderful father. Not my dad!"

John explained that her dad had slipped into unconsciousness shortly after Lucia left, meaning she was the last person who had the chance to talk with him while he was still coherent. Lucia took some small comfort in that.

Augustine had already heard the sad news and had come to console his sister. Together, they collapsed into each other's arms and tried to begin processing their father's death.

"God be praised, it was a peaceful death," Augustine said. "We can all take heart from that. He did not suffer much, as he was unconscious for the past few weeks. A fitting end for a man who lived in the service of others. Now he rests with the angels."

Lucia nodded slowly, as if in a trance.

"May those angels watch over us all," she said softly, adding, with a sad ghost of a smile, "I know Dad will."

# EPILOGUE

The funeral was in a small chapel near his home in Los Angeles. The chapel overflowed with people, which surprised his children, who knew him as a quiet man without much of a social life. Many of the mourners had served with Dr. Choi in the military, while others had known him as their doctor, as their friend, as someone they held in great respect—often a combination of all three.

The entire Choi and Hur families gathered to honor the life of a man revered wherever he went and wherever he practiced his own unique brand of medicine. His body was to be flown to Lexington, Kentucky, to be interred next to the burial plot of his wife, Lucia's mother, who had passed away on June 15, 1989. There, they would have another, smaller funeral service. His family flew to Lexington and waited for the coffin at the airport, but it never arrived. Who ever heard of a lost coffin? The coffin had changed flights in Atlanta, but from then on, the airline couldn't locate it. The funeral went on without a coffin.

Peter and Bobby were there, of course. Peter said little before, during, or after the ceremony because that was his way. Bobby, too, said little. It was as though he had retreated deep within himself and was going through the motions as if by rote. John took it stoically, like the man he was.

Several days later, they found the coffin. It was returned to the Choi and Hur families, and Dr. Choi was buried next to his wife. Though the loss of her father's coffin had been traumatic, Lucia wondered if perhaps the events had been her father's last lesson to his children: when something is lost, it can be restored with strength and perseverance.

Once all the funeral arrangements had been seen to and confirmed, John and Lucia returned to Austin to pick up the pieces from where they had left off before Lucia's surgery.

Dr. Choi's death had a profound effect on the family. Life continued as before, but with a less robust rhythm. It was as though there was an unwritten agreement among family members to maintain as steady a course as possible and not roil the waters. It was an interlude of introspection and calm, one that lasted many months, and one that the family had rarely experienced for any span of time since Bobby's accident.

Life has since returned to a semblance of normalcy—or as normal as is possible with the routine of such a family. John plays more golf these days, and he and Lucia are able to travel together.

Lucia has come to terms with God, and believes her cancer was a message from him that she needs to slow down. She promised her family, and herself, that she will not engage in the day-to-day operations of her new business venture in the anti-aging skin-care industry. True to her word, she passed ownership of the company to a third party. She has, instead, concentrated her efforts on crossing items off her bucket list and spending time with the family. Wonderful family vacations to Disneyland and Las Vegas have addressed both goals.

Peter still lives in Lubbock and enjoys the low-key but highly satisfying life he leads with his wife and two children. His relationship with his mother continues to grow more meaningful and substantive.

Dark clouds, however, continue to hover overhead. Although Bobby continues to be her primary concern and worry, Lucia has her own demons to confront on a daily basis. Although her operation was classified as a success, she is aware that cancer is a sticky and stubborn disease that is hard to totally obliterate. A recurrence in the future remains a possibility, and she is struggling to live and love with that reality hanging over her. In addition, she continues to battle issues with chronic leg pain, a longtime health issue that has returned in full force.

After a quarter-century of battling one foe after another, Bobby is finally coming to terms with himself and finding peace. The war is not yet won, however. Far from it. The rehab sessions continue, particularly in speech, physical, and behavioral therapies, and they likely will for the balance of his life. He continues to live alone in his condo, and while he is loath to admit it, he is still dependent on his mother logistically, emotionally, and financially. Even so, he is able to cope on his own, and he takes great pleasure in living independently. He continues to try to find himself, and searches for hidden talents. Every day, he writes and reads and learns more about himself and about the world around him. When he had his first book of poems self-published, it was a source of great pride to a forty-something man who, years earlier, had doctors in Lubbock give up on him. It took the power of love—the love of his parents and the love of Dr. Morledge and the medical team, who refused to give up on him and who unselfishly went the extra mile for him—to pull Bobby away from the edge of the abyss. He is now a vibrant contributor to society. This is all his parents ever wanted for their sons. It's what every parent wants for their children, no matter the challenges and handicaps those children might be confronting.

For Bobby and for every other member of the Choi and Hur families, all is fine. Despite the occasional setbacks, all is just fine. Dr. Choi's prophecy that all will be well is bearing fruit, and he leaves behind a legacy of perseverance, love, and, especially, the restorative value of hope. As Bobby's story proves, there is always hope, no matter how bleak or desperate the circumstances may seem. There is always hope

# ABOUT THE AUTHOR

Lucia Hur is a highly motivated and energetic woman with many interests and talents. Her list of titles and achievements includes mother, grandmother, wife, business woman, scientist, CEO/President of Hur Chemical Manufacturing & Contract formulation, and founder/CEO of Derma-Lucia Skinceuticals.

With a master's degree in marine exploration Geo Science, and over thirty years of experience in the chemical industry, she has dedicated her professional career to the science of formulation in the industrial public sector, as well as in the beauty industry. Her latest venture involves creating unique quality products for anti-aging regimen skincare.

She has dedicated her personal life to the betterment and enrichment of her family. She wrote *Perfect Love*, which first published in Korea, to cope and share the trauma that resulted from her son Bobby's car accident. She learned that her family's stumbling hurdles resonated with others regardless of cultures, race, and demographics as it has no boundaries.

She had promised herself to write her experiences in a book to share with others, which was on her bucket list priority # 1 for some time. She wants to reach out and share her experiences with the world. She hopes this story can serve as light in darkness to readers, and can inspire them to never give up.

Lucia lives and works in Austin, Texas, with her loving husband John. Her life motto is always do your best and enrich your soul!